MY WAR

Religion, Theology, and the Holocaust
Alan L. Berger, *Series Editor*

Other books in Religion, Theology, and the Holocaust

My War

MEMOIR OF A YOUNG JEWISH POET

Edward Stankiewicz

With a Foreword by Barbara Handler

Syracuse University Press

Library of Congress Cataloging-in-Publication Data

Stankiewicz, Edward.
     My war : memoir of a young Jewish poet / Edward Stankiewicz.—1st ed.
       p. cm.—(Religion, theology, and the Holocaust)
       ISBN 0–8156–0754–7
       1. Stankiewicz, Edward. 2. Jews—Poland—Biography. 3. Holocaust,
     Jewish (1939–1945)—Poland—Personal narratives. 4. Buchenwald
     (Concentration camp) I. Title. II. Series.
     DS135.P63 S7247 2002
     940.53'18'092—dc21
     2002011957

Der Tod ist ein Meister aus Deutschland
(Death is a master from Germany)

—Paul Celan

Edward Stankiewicz is professor emeritus of Slavic linguistics and literary theory at Yale University. He is the author of books and articles about Slavic and general linguistics, the history of linguistics, poetics, and Yiddish.

CONTENTS

FOREWORD

BARBARA HANDLER

Like many Jews, I am named after a dead relative, my father's younger sister, Bella. (We share the B.) My father, Edward Stankiewicz, last saw Bella, along with his mother, his younger brother Henry, and his older sister, Anna, in late September 1939, when he left German-occupied Warsaw for Lwów to continue his studies. All I really know about Bella is that she died in Hitler's war, a random fact absorbed sometime in childhood.

In kindergarten, I recall being disturbed by a classmate's outlandish claim that she had two sets of grandparents. That was as unlikely as saying she had two moms and two dads. I had one grandma and one grandpa—my mother's—and never questioned that that was how families were constructed. A person got one of everything: I had one sibling, my brother, Steve, one mother and father, one grandmother and grandfather, one uncle, one aunt, and one cousin.

However, as I grew older it dawned on me that other kids had scores of relatives. At Christmas they were busy buying them all presents, and they traveled to visit them; these relatives were not only grandparents, but aunts, uncles, cousins, second cousins twice removed, even godmothers. My mother had one brother from whom she was estranged, and after my mother's parents died, family meant just us: my parents,

Steve, and me. As the years passed, I felt increasingly alienated from my mostly Christian classmates with their large family reunions, good manners, and brightly lit Christmas trees crowded with piles of colorful gifts. They seemed so gay and wholesome and safe. Our apartment was gloomy at Christmas, with gray light falling on the menorah that sat on our kitchen table.

I don't remember ever not knowing of World War II, but I didn't know much about it. World War II was Hitler, Satan himself, a place called Buchenwald, and an attempt to kill all the Jews. My parents didn't discuss the war, feeling that as children we should be sheltered from knowing too much. When some girlfriends told me about the gas showers in the camps, it was like listening to horror stories told around the fire at summer camp. I didn't connect these things to my family, though I knew that Daddy sometimes woke screaming from nightmares about the Germans.

My brother and I loved hearing tales of when Daddy was our age. We begged for stories and heard about his sneaking out of his bedroom to study Latin by streetlight, of an amusing poem he'd written for his classmates, of a critique he'd made of a poem that was read at a literary gathering when he was seven or eight years old. My father was heroic without having gone through a concentration camp. He always said he would tell me about his war experiences when I turned eighteen. So the war remained an impression of incomprehensible but world-altering events and sketchy images of hollow-eyed men shuffling to their deaths in striped pajamas beneath blackened skies.

By the time I turned eighteen I was off to college and was very much living the life of an American student. I wore raggedy blue jeans, did yoga, ate with chopsticks, listened to the Watergate hearings, and worried about boys. I didn't talk to my parents very frequently. It was another twenty years before I finally sat down with my father on the living room couch with a tape recorder settled between us. I interviewed him about his experiences during the war and in two days accumulated five hours of tape. These I transcribed, put into a rough chronological order, and sent back to Dad to add to—which he did, bit by bit, as memories returned (and as he found time for the work). The result is this brief memoir to help us all remember, one more of the few but essential documents we have of how life was endured and how life endured during the Holocaust.

MY WAR

My High School Education

I was completing grade school in Warsaw in 1933 when Hitler came to power. His takeover of Germany came to hang like a dark cloud over the life of my family and our friends. Leaning politically to the Left, the adults talked endlessly about the dangers a Nazi Germany would present to democratic movements, to world peace, and especially to the Jews.

That year I entered the high school (*gymnasium*) from which I graduated in 1939. Graduation from the *gymnasium* was a major event in a young man's life because it determined his chances for a higher education. The certificate of maturity (*matura*) that one received after a series of exams was treated as a certificate of adulthood and an admission to the class of educated men. My class's year of "maturing" coincided with Germany's invasion of Poland and the outbreak of World War II. Whatever dreams we might have had about an active and committed life were shattered with the bombing of our city, the destruction of our homes, and the arrival of the German hordes. No one could have foreseen the nature of the terrors and the extent of the devastation ahead of us. However, the six years in high school, the years that coincided with Hitler's aggressions and the expansion of the Third Reich, were for me personally years of intense work and relative contentment.

I was a good student, though in some classes I got poor grades, mostly because I was bored with the subject or with the teachers. Some of them had little interest in teaching or were themselves bored with their subjects. Our biology teacher was a worn-out little creature with a squeaky voice and the eyes of a frog; all I remember of her classes was

1

the fun of looking through the microscope and the occasional vivisec-
tions we performed on beetles and frogs. Our teacher of logic, a wholesome young lady, was enthusiastic about her subject, but she presented it
in a way that put us all to sleep. As a result, I never discovered the beau-
ties of formal logic nor the mystery behind such formulas as *barbara* and
celarent. This was a pity, because interwar Poland had some of the finest
logicians of Europe. Math was taught by the director of the school, who
explained to us the basics of algebra and geometry while talking to the
blackboard, which he covered with fanciful figures and diagrams. What
he was saying to that blackboard was clearly not intended for the class.
Thus, I never mastered those two subjects either and missed the opportunity to go into mathematics. One year we had a substitute teacher who
presented trigonometry with zest and excitement, but after he left we
were stuck again with the lectures of the director. My indifference to his
lectures was aggravated by the sense that he did not like me (perhaps because of the leftist reputation of my father), a feeling I fully reciprocated.
Anyway, it was not easy to like him. He was a small, stooped, and impa-
tient man with squinting eyes and a sharp beak of a nose. His wife was
about two heads taller than he and a much-felt presence in the corridors
of the school, where she carried herself with an air of authority and command. She loved to admonish us if our uniforms were not properly
pressed or if we failed to greet her by clicking our heels and bending at
the waist.

Ours was a humanistic *gymnasium*, and in the humanities we had
some very fine teachers. At home we spoke Polish and Yiddish, and in
school I took Latin and German. We had a choice between French and
German, but I chose German in the hope that my knowledge of Yiddish
would facilitate the study of this language. Yiddish was helpful at the beginning, but later on it actually interfered with mastering German. For-
tunately, we had a tough teacher who saw to it that we did not
contaminate the language of Goethe with the guttural sounds and the
grammatical simplicities of Yiddish. Her training stood me in good stead
in my later encounters with the *Herrenvolk*, as well as in my later work.

The students and the administration of the school were all Jewish.

The professors, too, were mostly Jewish, but, like most of my classmates, they did not know a word of Yiddish and had not the slightest interest in Jewish culture. Yiddish was considered a jargon and its use a sign of lower-class upbringing. In Warsaw there were four or five *gymnasiums* for Jewish boys, and they were all thoroughly Polonized. Our patriotism was periodically bolstered by speeches and songs with which we celebrated the national holidays and was more explicitly articulated in our history classes, where we learned about our *hetmans* and kings, Poland's historical destiny, and its victories over the Teutons, the Turks, the Cossacks, the Swedes, and the Bolsheviks.

The state-owned Polish *gymnasiums* were not accessible to Jews, so middle-class Jewish boys could attend only Jewish schools. There was something paradoxical about our situation: on the one hand, we were expected to speak and behave as if we had imbibed Polish and Polish culture with our mother's milk, and, on the other hand, we were constantly reminded that we did not quite belong to this country because we were Jews. We were reminded of it in the streets, in the parks, on our trips, and by the very segregation of our schools. The university, too, discriminated against the Jews, especially after it introduced a *numerus clausus* and special benches for the Jews. We all knew that after graduation we would not be able to follow certain professions, at any rate not in Poland. Jewish boys who wanted to study medicine or architecture were shipped off to France, Belgium, or Italy. Despite Mussolini, Italy was the much-preferred country, and I knew some young men who came home for vacation from Bologna and Rome strumming their guitars and singing Italian songs. This whetted forever my appetite to see Italy, *das Land wo die Zitronen blühen,* though I had no desire to become a doctor or a lawyer. I wanted to be a teacher of Latin and Greek.

My Early Love of Latin

L atin was my favorite subject, and it took me early to the halls of Warsaw University, where the famous and by then ancient classical philologist Tadeusz Zielinski delivered his lectures in Latin. Particularly

well attended were his lectures on Greek mythology. I hardly understood half of what he was saying, but being in that lecture hall made me
feel like a grownup and a scholar. A minor incident ended it all. One
sunny morning a hooligan in a white student cap took a swing at me as I
was crossing the gates to the temple of learning. He obviously did not
like my face, a fact he corroborated with a colorful expletive. I realized
that Jews were not welcomed in this place. The irony of fate brought me
again to Warsaw University in 1992, but this time to lecture on a subject
never before taught at a Polish university, namely, the history of the Yiddish language.

My incident at the gates did not dampen my love of the classics. I
was fascinated not only by the mythology and poetry of the Romans,
but also by their allegedly dry grammar. I could not understand why
some students had trouble with the subject or found it a bore. For me it
was a source of fun and of minor discoveries that I paraded in front of the
class. Actually, I delighted not only in Latin but also in my Latin teachers. My favorite teacher was Walter Auerbach, by training a philosopher
and a classicist, who had come to us from Lwów. It was in Lwów that I
met him again after the outbreak of the war, and there that he was to play
a major role in my life. He was a tall, elegant man with a slightly stooped
posture and a shiny pate. But when he entered the class of sixteen- or
seventeen-year-old boys, greeting them with his broad smile and his
courteous "Witam panów" (I greet you, gentlemen), he won over the
hearts of the laziest students and the inveterate bullies of the school.
With the encouragement of Auerbach, I began to translate some of the
poetry we read, mostly the works of Virgil and Horace. I would recite
my translations at the beginning of the class, and though I was aware
that I made a mess of some of the poems (mostly because of my obses-
sion with the use of rhymes), I enjoyed the challenge and, no doubt, the
reputation of a translator-poet.

Before Auerbach, our Latin teacher was a Mr. Halpern, a Jew and an
officer of the Polish army, a combination not very common in prewar
Poland. In or out of his uniform, he cut an impressive figure. His classes
were models of discipline and, on his part, exercises in intimidation. If a

student got stuck on a passage or distorted the form of a Latin verb, Halpern would devastate him with his steely look, letting him squirm and twist in his seat as Halpern waited for the correct answer. His bearing and manner must have served him well in the Polish army, though I think that underneath this severe exterior was a warm and well-meaning man. He was particularly well disposed toward me, and I think that he expected me to follow in his footsteps (though not as an officer!). At the end of the school year, in 1937, he lent me a number of Latin books (Plautus, Catullus, Terence, etc.). That summer my family and I spent our vacation in a house with a leaking roof, and by chance I put the books in a corner under a leak. I was worried that this would be the end of my good relations with the professor. Either Halpern did not examine the returned books, or he pretended not to notice the damage. As it turned out, the books were of little use to me, because in the summer of 1937 I gave little thought to any study. This was indeed the most enjoyable summer of my youth.

The Summer of 1937

In the vicinity of our summer place there were five other students my age on vacation with their families—two boys and three girls. Two of them I had known in Warsaw. The father of one girl named Mańka was a labor leader and an acquaintance of my father. He stayed home most of the time because he was slowly dying of consumption. He died the following fall, and his funeral must have brought together all the labor unions of Warsaw. But during that summer the six of us had a grand time.

Almost every morning we would set out on a two- or three-mile hike to a beach along the Vistula. During the hike we sang songs in French, German, and Polish. Our basic repertory was provided by Julek, a boy with a deep baritone and a perfect ear. He could sing anything from the "Marseillaise" to the "Horst Wessel Lied," from the "Habanera" to the "Liebestod" of Isolde. We also knew a number of Polish folk songs and military marches. We sang all of them with great gusto. After a swim in the river and running around on the beach, we would return to our homes, only to meet again in the evening for volleyball and more singing. The hot afternoons were given to reading. That summer I read Tolstoy, Thomas Mann, Homer, and some Dickens for the first time (all in Polish). I got the greatest kick from *War and Peace*. Though I returned to Tolstoy later in my life, that first reading left an unforgettable impression. I recall the thrill I got from the description of the battles, the wanderings of Bezukhov, the withdrawal of *la grande armée*, and—for me the most memorable episode of the book—Natasha's dance. I also read some Soviet novels, which were repetitious and dull but were obligatory reading among my friends, particularly since in school they were treated as subversive fare. In my literature classes we read and discussed a number of foreign authors, but no teacher ever mentioned the names of Pushkin, Gogol, or Tolstoy. Things Russian were culturally taboo.

That summer I also had my first amorous adventure, if, indeed, it deserves such a name. Mańka was a pretty and well-developed girl. The two of us would sometimes take off by ourselves. Around us there were forests of pine trees and birches, secret paths, and clusters of huge mushrooms. Mańka wanted to be a doctor, and she considered it her duty to teach me the names of the trees, mushrooms, and birds. My interest in the subject was rather limited, and I must confess that I still cannot tell the difference between a finch and a sparrow, or a *Boletus edibilis* and a toadstool. We also took siestas under the big trees, listening to the birds and counting the drifting, puffy clouds. On some of these outings I brought along a copy of Homer to reciprocate for her lessons on nature. I would read to her some of my favorite passages, such as Hera's seduction of Zeus, Circe's love of Odysseus, his return to Ithaca, his flirtation with Nausikaa, and his killing of Penelope's suitors. On such occasions Mańka lay very close to me, and I could tell from her breathing that she took pleasure in the stories of seduction and of Odysseus's deceits. One day she came up with a poem of her own and said with a blush that she had written it for me. It was about a lilac branch leaning over a fence, the dark eyes of a young man, and the gentle touch of his hands. When I finished reading the poem, I felt awkward and embarrassed because it was apparent that I was both the cause and the object of this literary effort.

What was I to do? Admire the composition? Thank the author for her feelings? Kiss the girl? I had not kissed a girl before, and I was not going to do it now. In the end I said nothing. On the way back we were holding hands, but that was the end of our solitary walks.

After that summer our group fell apart. I came down with rheumatic fever, which kept me in bed for about three months. My friends tried to visit me, but I didn't want to be seen in my miserable state. After my recovery we met a few times, but then we became engrossed in our studies and stopped seeing each other. I still think of them from time to time. Oh, my sweet friends! Where are they now? Did any of them survive? Or did they all go up in smoke?

Exams and Graduation

I was the "official" school poet. In that capacity, I was expected to deliver an essay or a poem at the end of the school year. Before our graduation in June 1939, the school organized a ball to which we invited the graduating class of a girls' *gymnasium*. For the occasion, I delivered a poem called "A Day in School" in which I described the joys and miseries of our studies, our juvenile longings, and the charms and foibles of our teachers. What gave the poem its zest were the numerous quotations from great Polish poets. It was my first exercise in intertextuality. The poem was a hit, and it was circulated in the school weeks after the party. It pleased me that I was complimented even by the teachers I had lampooned. But my real reward was that on the night of the party I danced with some of the most beautiful girls in our schools.

At the end of June came our final exams. These finals were an ordeal comparable to the initiation rites practiced by some primitive tribes in Africa. Though no one died in the process, all were submitted to the same grueling test, the rite of passage that enabled one to seek a higher education. Failure to pass not only denied a person this right but also left him covered with shame for the rest of his life.

There were written exams in Polish and German and oral exams in Latin and history. In history, I knew only one subject: the Italian Renaissance. Because of my reputation as a classicist, I had reason to believe that the teacher would ask me questions about Greek or Roman history. But both of these subjects I knew only in a vague and haphazard way. I had trouble with the dates of the great battles and with the deeds of the many tyrants and emperors. The fact is that the whole political history we'd been taught about these countries seemed to me pointless and a bore; but I had strong feelings about the Italian Renaissance and found it eminently worthy of study. I liked its discovery of the individual, the growth of industries, its colorful cities, the conquests of a new language and literature, and, above all, the explosion of the visual arts. My interest in the subject was especially whetted by my reading of the book by its great historian, Jakob Burkhardt. During the exam, the teacher handed out, as in a lottery, little folded slips of paper with a question written inside. And, lo and behold, the question I received was on the Italian Renaissance. It must be that the teacher had read my mind or had planned to slip me this question all along. Needless to say, I did pretty well.

After the exams we were lined up in a row and the director of the school moved along it, congratulating each student. When he came up to shake my hand, he informed me that the administration of the *gymnasium* had decided to award me a fellowship for all four years of study at the university. This was the high point of my student career. I was so excited that I ran all the way home to share the news with my mother. Unfortunately, I've never had the chance to thank the school for its generosity. The building has remained, but the school and its teachers have long since disappeared.

But to tell the truth, it was not my ambition to become a scholar. My secret dream was to become a part-time teacher of Latin and a full-time poet and painter. I had doodled and painted as far back as I can remember. During my years at the *gymnasium* I used to do the sets for our theatrical productions, and I offered the school several portraits of Józef Piłsudski. It was a cinch to paint our glorious marshal with his stern profile, his stiff, short-cropped hair, his long Polish mustache, and his ribboned high collar. In my early school years, I would also set out with my paints and easel to Warsaw's Old Town, with its colorful narrow streets and high-gabled medieval houses. These escapades were not without incident, because the local ragamuffins did not like Jewish-looking boys on their turf. They would throw stones at me or turn my easel over. But when I started writing poetry, I began to hope that, like a Norwid or a Wyspiański, I would one day combine the professions of poet and painter. I hardly could have imagined that my artistic skills would one day get me into a more serious business, the business of a forger.

I spent the summer of 1939 with my family in the countryside not far from Warsaw. When I was a little boy, we used to go on vacation to Kazimierz, a little town on the Vistula and the birthplace of my mother. My memory of Kazimierz is of a bustling little town emerging as from a dreamlike fog. The town was predominantly Jewish, and it was famous for the palace of Esterka, the Jewish mistress of Kazimir the Great, to whom many a Jewish writer had dedicated his literary efforts. Her palace was now a ruin, but Jews with side locks and beards crowded the marketplace and narrow streets of the town, as they must have done when King Kazimir brought them to Poland. Not far from the marketplace was the Vistula, and on some nights the Jews would gather along its shores to pray in the light of a full moon. Around the town there were high hills, and my father and I would sometimes get up to the top of one. We would sit there, taking in the silvery sliver of the river and the sight of the dark forests stretching out in the distance. Kazimierz had been a great attraction for painters, and I told myself that when I grew up I would return to the birthplace of my mother at least once a year. I returned to it only once, twenty years after the war, to visit my friend, the Polish novelist Maria Kuncewicz, and I was anxious to get away as soon as I had come. The once busy marketplace was deserted, and the hunched-over houses exuded the melancholy of a cemetery. The hustle and bustle of the former Jewish life was gone, and the guttural voices that had reverberated in the streets had been silenced. The silence of the vanished Jews echoes throughout Kazimierz more than in any other shtetl of Poland.

The Outbreak of the War

At the end of August 1939, we heard over the radio the news of the Molotov-Ribbentrop Pact, and soon afterward the Germans attacked Poland. We decided to return to Warsaw, because we didn't know what might happen and we were afraid of being cut off. Very few people had cars, and the best we could do was to rent a horse-drawn wagon on which we put my sick brother, our furniture, and our books. My younger brother had been immobilized for several years because of an accident he suffered as a young boy in school. His spine had been broken against a windowsill, and he was paralyzed up to his chest.

On the second or third day after our return to Warsaw, I found myself in a Polish neighborhood far from home when the German planes came zooming down over the town. The planes were dropping bombs, but there was fear that they were spreading gas. I ran into a Polish house. We all expected to be poisoned. A few days later the Germans bombed the Jewish neighborhood during the solemn holidays of Rosh Hashana and Yom Kippur. The houses were set on fire by a barrage of incendiary bombs.

As a result of the bombing we had to move. We went to the apartment of the friends with whom we had spent the summer in the country. But soon Warsaw was again under bombardment, and we spent most of our time down in the basement. One day I went out to find bread with my friend, the son of the family we stayed with. We were standing in line to a bakery when shrapnel began to fall. Instinctively, I hid behind my friend. When I realized what I was doing, I felt cowardly and deeply ashamed, and I told myself that I must get away, that I must leave this hungry and ravaged city. The wounds of war were visible everywhere. People were searching for their belongings in burnt-out houses, streetcars stood frozen in their tracks, horses with open bellies were lying in the middle of the streets, and men with hatchets and knives were cutting them up for chunks of meat.

One incident remains forever engraved on my mind. One day we were under heavy shelling and had no time to make it to the basement.

We remained in the gate of the house; like many European entrance gates, it was enormous. We huddled in the entrance because the arches of the gate were reputed to provide the best protection from the shells. My brother was in a wheelchair and my father stood near him. Suddenly the house shook, and I was sure we were going to be buried under a pile of rubble. When I opened my eyes, I saw my father bent over my brother to shelter him from the falling bricks. The ceiling of the gate didn't give, but we were all shaken up.

Warsaw was under siege for about three weeks. I didn't see the Germans marching into town, but suddenly they were all over. I don't remember many details of that period, but I know that there was hunger, plunder, and death. One day I was caught by a German soldier, who gave me a broom and ordered me and a group of other men to sweep the street. After that incident, I told myself that it was time to leave, to get away from the German plague. By that time the Soviets had taken eastern Poland, while the Germans occupied the western part all the way to the river Bug. The Russians laid claim to eastern Poland under the pretext that it was ethnically Ukrainian and Byelorussian territory. After the war these regions were indeed incorporated into the Soviet Union; now they are a part of Ukraine and Belarus.

Good-bye to Warsaw

After the traumas of the bombings and my street-sweeping incident, I was ready to leave for the Soviet-occupied zone. I reckoned that I could not be of any help to my parents, and I knew that under the Germans I had no future. I was eighteen and had my *matura* and the determination to go on with my studies. On the Russian side there were schools, universities, and jobs.

My father arranged my trip to the East in the company of some older men whom he knew from his connections with the labor unions. My parents did not like the idea of my leaving, but they didn't oppose it. Like me, they believed, rather naïvely, that on the Russian side things would be zipping along. In fact, when I crossed the frontier and saw the first company of Russian soldiers with their pointed hats and red stars, I was ready to embrace them as liberators and friends; it was only the exotic faces of the Mongols and Kalmucks that gave me some pause.

I said good-bye to my parents, not knowing when or whether we would meet again. We knew that this war would be meaner and crueler than any before. The First World War was sometimes recalled by my parents, but from a distance of twenty years it appeared to them a relatively benign affair. People could move back and forth over vast areas together with, and even against, the movements of the troops. There had been no mass massacres of civilians, and, at least in Poland, the German army behaved no worse than any other occupying force. In some parts of Poland the Germans had established hospitals and fed the hungry, and they did not single out the Jews for special treatment. They certainly had a better reputation than the Cossacks, who plundered the countryside, murdered the Jews, and ravished the women. That's why some older people in Warsaw believed that under the German occupation things couldn't be too bad. After all, they would argue, the Germans were a civilized nation, the nation of Beethoven and Goethe. Of course, one should have realized, especially after reading *Mein Kampf*, that Hitler had set the stakes for a completely new kind of war. Yet even some sober people treated with skepticism his triple threat of destroying Bolshevism, enslaving the Slavs, and exterminating the Jews. He fulminated against so many enemies that at first he was taken for a clown, a madman bound for destruction of his *Volk* by his own megalomania. Eventually this did happen, of course, but by God, at what a price!

Before the war, even some sober-thinking Jews were inclined to believe that Hitler was a great man. After all, he had put his people to work, had built bridges and highways, had put new cars on the roads, and had liquidated the squabbles of the political parties. Our teacher of German, a no-nonsense type of Jewish woman named Papierna, admired all things German, including the Führer. "No matter what we may think of Hitler's ideology," she would enlighten us in class, "the fact is that the man is a genius." All over Europe and outside the very walls of our school fascism was showing its hideous mug, yet people refused to see it for what it was.

My history textbooks had a chapter on fascism that was full of babblings about racial purity, Italian syndicates, and new highways but devoid of information about the new concentration camps, the burning of books, and the suppression of freedoms. Poland was flirting with the Nazis (Goering and some other German big shots had come on a hunting visit to the Białowieża Forest), and the Polish anti-Semites became more aggressive and shrill by the day. Jews were attacked in the press and in the streets. Even some of my family's Polish friends (unfortunately, mostly leftists) warned us that our future in Poland looked bleak. When I confessed to my friend Wanda Serwacka, a highly educated lady who had been living for years with a Jew, that I intended to become a poet, she shook her head in disbelief, looking at me with pity. "Why the devil would you want to do that?" she said. "You will be better off, and safer, if you become a shoemaker or a plumber. Don't you know how they treat poets of Jewish origin in this country? Wasn't Słonimski publicly slapped in the face? And do not the Endeks [the acronym for the National Democrats] say daily that Tuwim has contaminated our beautiful Polish tongue?"

Our sense of isolation from the Christian world had become ever more pronounced, even though the Jews and the gentiles of Warsaw had been separated from each other for centuries by culture, language, and residence. Though the Jews theoretically could live in any part of town, only a small number of the more prosperous Jews, including the professionals, lived in the Polish neighborhoods; most of them (and Warsaw counted about half a million Jews) were concentrated in the areas of Zamenhofa, Nowolipki, and Gęsia (the street near the Jewish cemetery). The closest contacts we had with the gentile world were through the Polish janitors and housemaids. The latter had not only learned to speak Yiddish but often remained the only dependable friends and protectors of the Jews.

One early October morning, while my siblings were still asleep, my mother took me to the place where the group leaving Warsaw was to meet. Her face was yellow, and she looked haggard and tired. She wore my father's overcoat, appearing lost and forlorn in the cold morning fog.

We embraced while she wiped away the tears from her eyes. We turned away from each other in silence because the words got stuck in our throats. I never saw her again, my beautiful and much-tested *mater dolorosa*.

After a few days of marching, our group reached the German-Russian border. We decided to stay overnight in a nearby village, for we were told that the Germans arrested or sent back the people who were trying to cross the frontier. We found lodging in a peasant's barn and were getting ready to stretch out for the night when we were visited by a German soldier. "Where are you going," he asked, "and what is your business?" I was the only one who spoke German, and I promptly made up a story that we were planning to join relatives on the Soviet side. He demanded to see our papers and what we carried in our bundles. After a perfunctory glance, he gave us back the papers (they were all in Polish) but asked us to hand over our money and our watches. He took whatever we gave him and disappeared as quickly as he had come. I thought that we had gotten off scot-free but my companions took it very hard. They thought they'd been robbed by an ordinary bandit. One wanted to go back to Warsaw, to his wife; another cried quietly that he had lost all his money; a third began chewing on his sausages and bread; I developed a high fever. But in the morning my fever was gone and I took command of the group. With the help of the peasant's son, a boy of about twelve, we found a way through the woods that took us over to the other side. In no time we were at the edge of a little town, where we saw the first detachment of Soviet soldiers. At this point, I said good-bye to my companions and proceeded by train to the town of Bialystok.

Bialystok had long had a sizeable Jewish population, but now it was teeming with displaced, confused, and homeless Jews. There was hardly room for them in the schools, synagogues, alleyways, and private homes where they tried to establish provisional quarters. There were Jews of many stripes: Hasidim with side locks and felt hats, Bundists, Communists, Polish-speaking intellectuals, and laborers speaking a crude Warsaw Yiddish. It was as if a cross-section of Polish Jewry had descended upon this dusty and God-forsaken town. All seemed to be in a hurry, yet they did not know exactly where to go. Some were aiming for Lithuania, which was still an independent state; some wanted to go deep into Russia; some planned to go all the way to Japan; and some packed up and returned home. I decided to go to Lwów, the hometown of several of my teachers and the only town that was likely to have a university.

Lwów

L wów has four official names: its Latin name is Leopolis, in Polish it is known as Lwów, in Ukrainian as L'viv, and in Russian as L'vov (henceforth I shall refer to it as Lwów). The Jews of Lwów knew it by its German name, Lemberg. In 1939, it was still a very Polish town and I remember it above all as Lwów. It was a beautiful town, tracing its history to the early Middle Ages. During the many years of Austrian occupation it acquired a strong Austrian appearance, with baroque churches, heavy-set houses, pompous statues, and a beautiful park overlooking the city.

At the beginning I stayed in a hostel for refugees. I took the entrance exam to the university in the hope of taking up the study of classics. I wrote a long-winded essay about my love of Greek and Latin poetry, but it didn't help. As I found out after the exam, I was rejected not because of the essay, but because the university did not accept refugees. To make some money, I took a job at the railway station unloading coal from a freight train. It was a backbreaking job, and after a few days I quit. I figured there must be easier ways of earning a living.

After some searching, I enrolled in an institute that was supposed to train public school teachers. The school was divided into Ukrainian and Jewish departments. There was no Polish department, because Polish had ceased to be an official language. In the Jewish department, the language of instruction was Yiddish. The peculiar thing about that department was that the teachers hardly knew any Yiddish; the Jewish intelligentsia of Lwów was thoroughly assimilated and spoke only Polish. The students who knew Yiddish were mostly from the shtetls of Galicia and Volynia. The Yiddish textbooks were imported from Kiev or Moscow. I was one of the few who knew some literary Yiddish, and it was in that school that I began to compose Yiddish poems. I had no intention of making a career of it; I did it to entertain my classmates and to satisfy the needs of the school newspaper.

My Teachers

I had three favorite teachers in that school. One of them was its direc-tor, a former principal of a Hebrew *gymnasium* and a labor Zionist. Now he had been forced to give up his teaching of Hebrew and deny his former Zionism as a youthful aberration. He taught several courses and made a valiant effort to lecture in Yiddish. Two years later, when the Germans established the Lwów ghetto, he became a policeman. One winter day when I came back from work, I saw him with twelve other po-licemen strung up on balconies and on several lampposts. Their faces were blue and their tongues stuck out, while their bodies slowly turned in the chilly breeze. I clenched my fists and I swore that one day we would avenge them, though I knew full well that that day would never come.

Another one of my teachers was the Yiddish poet Deborah Vogel. She taught modern Yiddish literature, though the only languages she was able to speak were Polish and German. She had written some exper-imental Yiddish poetry one could not easily understand. On top of that, she had written several Polish and German essays on avant-garde art, which she had published in philosophical journals and which, curiously enough, did not much differ from her poems. While she was my teacher, I read only one or two of her works. I could not say that I understood them, but it pleased me that she liked the poems I published in our school newspaper. After the war Deborah Vogel came again to my at-tention in connection with Bruno Schulz, her lifelong friend. The work of Bruno Schulz received some acclaim in the 1980s, when his stories and drawings were published in Poland and in the United States. He was killed by the Nazis in Drohobycz, the town in which he was born and which he described in brilliant and intriguing surrealistic prose.

Another teacher I was fond of was Ola Heller. She talked to the class in Polish because she did not know a word of Yiddish. Ultimately it did not matter, because she was our art teacher. The two of us hit it off from the start: I liked her classes and she liked my drawings. She was a very pretty woman of about thirty or thirty-five. One nice day she invited me to come to her house for tea. She told me that she was living with her husband and a sister-in-law, a certain Dr. Groebel. It was the first time I was invited to a local middle-class home, and, self-conscious about my frayed winter coat and worn-out shoes, I made myself look as natty as I could for the visit. Imagine my surprise when the door to Dr. Groebel's apartment was opened by none other than my Latin teacher from Warsaw, Professor Auerbach. He was Ola's husband. From that time on I paid frequent visits to Dr. Groebel's apartment, which I came to know more intimately in the winter of 1941, during the German occupation of Lwów. But that was a later and trickier phase of my life, a life of fears and uncertainties. In the meantime I felt lucky that two of my favorite teachers, Auerbach and his wife, were local citizens to whom I could turn in case of need.

The Dormitory

In the late fall of 1939 I moved into a dormitory provided by the school. It was located in a peeling, grim building with no showers and no hot water. The place provided our two daily meals, breakfast and dinner, but its principal feature was its abominable squalor. The director of the dormitory, a warm and sophisticated woman, apparently had enough money to employ cooks but not janitors. Consequently, we were permanently sinking in garbage. Even at dinnertime we could watch the mice scurrying around for food. Outside the building rats did the same. The toilets were overflowing, and we literally stepped in human waste when we used them. One of the tribulations of my life in the dormitory was that even in the bitter winter I had to look for one of the toilets located in the neighboring courtyards. After a while I got to know all of the more or less acceptable outhouses. As a rule these were wooden contraptions with no seats and wide cracks in the walls, but they provided relative privacy and, on windy days, a whiff of fresh air.

Another source of misery was the lack of showers. I could get myself to a public bath, but the city baths smelled of stagnant water, and I had to pay good money for a towel and soap. To top it all, the winter of 1940 was one of the coldest winters in anyone's memory. My first year under Soviet rule thus became a test of youthful endurance. There were few services, mountains of filth, and no money. I consoled myself that I had a roof over my head, that I had enough to eat, and that I did not have to face any Germans. For a Jewish refugee from Warsaw, that seemed to be plenty.

The bitter cold of that winter and the lack of hygiene caused some severe problems. Students slept in their sweaters, covered themselves with their winter coats, and stuffed newspapers or straw into their shoes. Despite such measures, many came down with colds and stayed for days in their beds. Luckily there were no lice, but in the early spring most residents of the dormitory came down with scabies. I too contracted it, but being ashamed to stay in the dormitory, I took myself to one of the local hospitals. I spent about a week under perfect care, whiling the time away with the poetry of Pindar and Sappho. I returned to the dormitory a cleaner and better man.

Despite the squalor of our place, we had frequent visitors. They were Soviet soldiers garrisoned in or around Lwów who came to flirt with our girls. Most of them were friendly, outgoing fellows, speaking a corrupt Russian and flashing smiles at us that narrowed to a slit their Mongolian or Kalmuck eyes. "U nas vse est" (we have everything), they liked to brag, while stories were circulated in Lwów that the soldiers would sell anything to obtain a watch, and that they washed their faces in toilet bowls because they mistook them for wash basins. I don't know about the girls, but I came to like their banter and easy manner—until a few months later, that is, in the spring of 1940, when they appeared with heavy trucks to round up and deport into Russia thousands of refugees and other undesirable elements. When they came knocking at our doors, dragging women and children into the trucks, they looked to me like their medieval ancestors, who had poured forth from the Asiatic steppes to wreak havoc in the civilized West.

Making Ends Meet

Our monthly stipends were absurdly small, and to survive I had to earn some money. At one point I got a job as a tutor. One of my students was a sickly boy from a middle-class Jewish family who could not attend school. Before the arrival of the Soviets the family had owned several public baths, but after they were expropriated, the father of the boy was given the position of supervisor. In this capacity he was selling tickets to the baths and renting out towels and soap, though he spent most of his time reading novels and complaining about the Soviet regime. It was a miracle that he did not wind up in jail.

Off and on I earned some money by painting portraits of the Soviet leaders. The demand for such portraits would increase before official holidays, especially the one celebrating the October Revolution. To enhance the significance of such events, the state had ordained to exhibit, in the tradition of the Byzantine Church, icons of its dead and living high priests. These came in the form of portraits of diverse size: the more important the priest, the bigger the portrait. The usual portrait was the size of a window or door, while the large ones could cover the facade of a building. Painting the Soviet leaders was a lucrative business, and it was guarded by guilds of professional artists with good connections at the top. But occasionally the demand surpassed the supply, and smaller enterprises that could not afford the fees set by the guilds settled for cheaper and smaller products. That was my opening. I searched out directors of smaller enterprises, offering them a reasonable price for my wares. The work was fairly mechanical, for it was based on photographs or portraits that had official blessing. Easiest to paint, and always in demand, were the portraits of Lenin and Stalin: the first had a bald head and a goatee, while the second had big eyebrows and a hefty moustache. But the business was not without risk, for if the portraits were not in keeping with the tastes of the people who had ordered them, they refused to pay. They could always claim that the portraits did not do justice to the splendor of the subjects, whereas I could hardly take them to court. After a while I realized that the secret to success was not to produce an exact copy but rather to rejuvenate or embellish the original. In the end my attempt to open up the market fizzled out; the risk of not being paid was not worth all that effort.

The Deportations

The masses of refugees who wound up in Lwów were a headache for the Soviet administration. As in Białystok, they milled around the soup kitchens, set up camp in schools and synagogues, and slept at the railway station and in the entrances to private homes. Some sought refuge in the smaller towns, others wandered around the countryside, and some returned to the German zone. However, in January and February 1940 the Soviet government, perhaps Stalin himself, decided to solve the refugee problem with a single stroke: all refugees, including women and children and thousands of Jews, were identified as potential spies and were therefore subject to deportation to the remotest corners of the Soviet state. The deportations began around January and continued in two or three waves during February and March. Russian soldiers showed up with heavy trucks in the middle of the night and took away everyone who could not prove that he or she had lived in the western Ukraine before the war. The soldiers moved from house to house, checking papers and dragging entire "illegal" families into the trucks. The nights were filled with the crying of children, the screaming of women, and the yelling of soldiers.

When the deportations began, I was sure that my life as a free agent in Lwów was over. I certainly had no desire to wind up somewhere in the south with the Tajiks or near the White Sea with the reindeer. I was still hoping to enter the university and did not care to leave Lwów, with its sophisticated, though too often snobbish, people. I was also aware that some refugees were being permitted to stay. Among them were writers, well-known former Communists, and people with connections (*protekcja*). However, some prominent leftists wound up in jail. The system was both capricious and sloppy, and no one bothered to explain its moves. But one thing was certain: it treated its faithful no better than its enemies. As a result, people on either side often found themselves in the same gulag or cell.

I tried to use whatever connections I had to get permission to remain in Lwów. By that time I was acquainted with several Yiddish poets, who liked the things I had shown them. I told them how anxious I was to continue my studies. About this matter I was not quite sincere, but I had to present some good reasons to stay. Since none of the writers I talked to had received a university education, they were not too impressed by my plea. But even if they had wanted to help, a good word on my behalf coming from a Jewish writer would have had the power of a postprandial burp. The Jewish writers of Lwów must have been very, very small fry in the eyes of the regime. The fact is that before their withdrawal the Soviet authorities had helped most Polish and Ukrainian writers get away, whereas all Jewish writers I knew got stuck in Lwów, to be annihilated by the Nazis and their Ukrainian cohorts.

My chance to remain in Lwów was resolved in a simple and completely fortuitous way. The director of my dormitory had often talked to me about my family in Warsaw, about my school, and about my plans. She also knew enough Yiddish to appreciate my literary efforts. From the very beginning she treated me as a friend. One fine morning before one of the massive deportations, she handed me a document stating that for the last five years I had been living in Złoczów, a town not far from Lwów. Thus I was saved; I was not dispatched to Siberia to dig ditches or to cut down trees. Alas! Two years later the joy I had felt for escaping deportation to the Soviet hinterland was poisoned by the belief that I might have been better off had I not been saved by my noble benefactor.

In the meantime my education in the pedagogical institute was coming to an end. In June 1940, after eight months of half-hearted and make-believe study, my classmates and I were going to get a diploma entitling us to teach in a Jewish public school wherever the government would deem to send us. Thus we could pay back the state for the gift of a free education. However, the last thing I wanted was to be a schoolteacher in a provincial shtetl teaching Yiddish to eight- or ten-year-old children. God knows, I did not go to the institute to end up in some hole of a town, but rather to gain a roof over my head and to receive two meals a day.

The graduation ceremony came around with a dinner and speeches, all in Ukrainian! We were told about our duties to the Soviet fatherland and about our good luck at being in the vanguard of socialist culture. After the vacations we were to come back to report for assignment to our new jobs. Once school was over the dormitory was closed, and most of my colleagues went home to their families in the shtetls of Galicia and Volynia. Finding myself without a base, I went to Rovno, where my father had found a job with a construction company. But I stayed there only a few weeks, because other than a part-time job, there was nothing for me to do in that half-forgotten, dusty, and sleepy town.

My Family

In the fall of 1939 I was still in touch with my family in Warsaw. I especially valued a photograph I received of my mother and two sisters. All three looked young and healthy, but they did not write how and what they were doing. Some time in December I received the news that my brother had died. He was sixteen, but being paralyzed he had needed special care, which neither my mother nor my sisters were able to provide. So he died. When I got the news I felt shattered. It was one of the coldest nights of the year, but I could not go back to the dormitory. I hid behind the gate of a house and cried. It was as if I had just discovered what he had meant to me all those past years. Later on when we saw people dying each day, we did not cry; we just waited our turn to follow in the same way. In the winter of 1939, one could still cry.

After my brother's death my father left Warsaw too. With the Germans in town his business was obviously finished. He settled in Rovno, a town near the old Polish-Russian border. As a young man, my father had been busy in politics and in the Jewish labor unions. But sometime in the thirties things began to go wrong. He seemed to have lost his faith and became an entrepreneur. He joined forces with a Mr. Burgin, a respected religious Jew with a patriarchal white beard and a ready wit. In 1941, I ran into two of his sons, twins, who had come over to Lwów and who got me a job in a Polish restaurant. Unfortunately, that connection ended on a sour note. Mr. Burgin and my father were buying and refurbishing old houses, including synagogues. My father took me along to some of these places, where I watched with fascination as Jewish painters on high scaffolds decorated the shuls with fantastic lions, imaginary deer, red oxen, multicolored birds, and magic letters. The synagogues have long since been destroyed, but the animals have miraculously survived—in the paintings of Chagall. I too dreamed of painting such lovely animals and colorful birds.

I never learned what kind of job my father found in Rovno, but apparently he was hanging on. Several times he came to visit me in Lwów, where he had some business. He stayed over with friends on Leona Sapiehy, one of the major thoroughfares of the city. The house and the people he stayed with I got to know pretty well, because this was the place I ran to after the outbreak of the German-Russian war and the bombing of my dormitory. During the summer of 1940, I went to see my father in Rovno, where he found me a temporary job as a house and sign painter. But Rovno did not offer much to keep me there. I lost all contact with my father after the arrival of the Germans. I was never able to find out when or how he died, but I was sure that he had no way of leaving with the Soviets. In the small towns the Germans gave the Jews no quarter; thus my father must have perished with the rest of the Rovno Jews in the summer of 1941, that is, right after the arrival of the German troops.

The University

At the end of the summer I applied again to the university, taking the entrance exam for the department of classics. This was a highly undernourished department. It had only three applicants and was happy to admit anyone who came along. The study of classics was definitely not a hot item. Thus I attained my goal—I became a student of classical philology.

However, my enthusiasm for my studies fizzled out almost the moment I was accepted. For one thing, the university itself was in a state of transition. Though the professors of classics were the same as before the war and their courses were held in Polish, the administration of the university was Ukrainian, and Ukrainian became the official language. In addition, a number of instructors were transplanted from Kiev to teach brand-new courses, such as Marxism-Leninism and Ukrainian literature, all delivered in Ukrainian, a language few of us knew or cared to know. Even the Latin classes turned out to be a bore. The professor, an old-fashioned pedant and a believer in the division of departmental functions, was annoyed by my questions about the origin of certain grammatical forms, advising me to turn with such questions to the authority on comparative grammar down the corridor in room such-and-such. "Our business," he said with solemnity, "is not historical grammar but the correct translation of a Latin text." There was nothing to warm the heart in that department, and I began to devote more and more time to reading and to writing poetry.

In the meantime the government had forgotten about its investment in my pedagogical training and my obligation toward the Soviet state. It was now covering my maintenance at the student house of the university. This was a bigger place than my previous dormitory, and much cleaner. The students belonged to various departments and were of several nationalities. In the hallways one could hear Ukrainian, Polish, Russian, and Yiddish. The student house did not serve food, but we received coupons and a monthly stipend that kept us on a level with the lowest members of the proletarian class. As before, I tried to supplement my stipend with occasional little jobs.

In exchange for the benefits it heaped upon us, the state demanded not only that we study and pass the exams, but also that we participate in interminable meetings. These were generally opened by the rector of the university and followed by speeches given by deans and invited guests—all this being a part of our political education. The most amazing thing about the speeches was the degree of obsequiousness and genuflection toward the regime. Here were apparently healthy and rational men performing grotesque gyrations and pirouettes in praise of the state and its Great Leader. One could only wonder whether the founders of socialism could ever have imagined the degree of abasement and hypocrisy their ideology would demand.

The Writers' Club

Having lost interest in classical studies, I spent a great deal of time in the library acquiring a literary education. I read Polish and Ukrainian writers and the works of Soviet and local Yiddish poets. Since Polish was not recognized as an official language, there seemed to be no future in writing Polish verse. After my experience in the Yiddish pedagogical school, I decided to try my luck in Yiddish. I knew enough Yiddish to compose a poem, and I was encouraged to go on writing in Yiddish by Shudrikh, one of the local poets I had met when I was still in the pedagogical school. Through him I got to know several other Jewish writers, who would meet almost daily in the Writers' Club. As it turned out, these connections helped save my life. During the interminable raids on the ghetto, some prominent Lwów Jews conceived a plan to protect Jewish artists and writers by offering them jobs in the Judenrat (the Kehillah). Thanks to my feeble products, I found myself included in that group.

In the Writers' Club I also met some luminaries of Polish literature who were—or had become—enthusiastic admirers of the Soviet state. They expressed their admiration in public lectures in which they explained that European culture had now shifted to the east of the Bug (the river separating the new Soviet and German states) and in which one heard more and more often the name of "the genius of mankind" and "the sun of our Soviet homeland," Josif Vissarionovich Stalin.

Shudrikh became a close friend. He would read his poems to me during the many hours I spent in his home. They were full of late autumn leaves, of sick birds, and of a love that is gone and wears down the heart. He was, in fact, a lonely man without any visible family or friends. Through him I also met a charming Jewish writer, Samuel Imber, and his wife, a concert pianist. Imber was the exact opposite of Shudrikh. While

Shudrikh had never been outside of his native Lwów, Imber had seen a number of countries. He had spent some years in Palestine and in America and had written poetry and essays in several languages. While Shudrikh could write only in Yiddish, Imber was an excellent Polish stylist and the author of a biting tract, "Asy czystej rasy" (Aces of a pure race), in which he attacked Polish anti-Semitism. I had a feeling that Imber clung to Shudrikh because as a former Zionist and world traveler he was not trusted by the regime, whereas Shudrikh, as an old-time leftist and proletarian poet, enjoyed considerable respect in the Writers' Club. Still, he was a decent man and a tender, lyrical poet.

At the university I also met several young Polish poets, most of them a few years older than I. They were mostly Jews, but Polish was the only language they knew and could write in. Two of them were to play an important role in my life under the Germans. Piotr Rawicz was a student of Sanskrit, something of a mystic, and an admirer of the Russian futurists. He himself wrote arcane, experimental poetry that I loved to hear him recite, but that I could hardly understand. The other was Frank Stiffel, a student of French literature and a lover of the French symbolists. He translated some of their poems into Polish, but was secretive about his own writings. All of us formed a circle in which we talked about literature and read our own writings. Rawicz and Stiffel survived the war and have written several gripping books about their experiences.

The high point of my career as an aspiring poet was when I was invited to give a public reading of my poetry in the Writers' Club. I expected an indifferent reception, because Yiddish poetry was hardly a big drawing card and I was practically unknown. The greater and more pleasant was my surprise, therefore, when several of my poems were discussed and singled out for praise. Shudrikh, who had arranged my appearance, was delighted with my success. He had known, he said, that he was betting on a good horse. In the spring of 1941, I also met several Soviet Yiddish poets who came on a visit to Lwów. I spent a whole day with Dovid Hofshteyn, showing him "my" town and reciting to him a few of his own poems that I loved. I still think that Hofshteyn was one of the finest Yiddish poets to emerge in the Soviet period, even though he had to make a number of compromises with the regime. On the other hand, he had spent some years in Palestine and was more traveled and better educated than most Soviet Yiddish writers. I also met Perets Markish, who moved and talked like a movie actor. No longer young, he paraded a mop of black hair and a beautiful Greek profile. He was certainly the most handsome and talented of the Soviet Yiddish poets, despite a rambunctious futurist phase and a readiness to serve the powers that be. I read to him a few of my poems, and all he had to say to me was "goden" (will do), the Russian word for recruits suitable for the draft. Among other visitors, we had the Communist firebrand, Itsik Fefer. He was the opposite of Markish, both in looks and in quality. He was puny and unappealing, with a fixed smirk on his face. He drummed out his poems as if to the beat of a military march, and he remained until the end the most servile and reptilian sycophant of the state. On August 12, 1952, before his very execution, he still hoped to save his life by betraying his fellow writers.

New and exciting possibilities seemed to have opened to me. Though I never intended to become a Yiddish poet (for one thing, I never mastered the fine points of the language, the so-called *kleyne pintelekh*), I sent my stuff to the Yiddish literary journal in Kiev. I got a letter from the editor in chief, Kvitko, that he liked my poems, though he found them wanting because of their lack of "Soviet content." He would be glad to publish them, he wrote, if I would add material reflecting "our" Soviet reality. I never got around to doing so, and thus I never got to see the fruits of my labor in print.

The Germans in Lwów

On June 22, 1941, the Germans announced their attack against the Soviet Union by bombing the city of Lwów. One of their first targets was my student house. When the ceiling began to fall, I ran out of the house. Under my feet I saw a severed hand and, at a certain distance from it, a head with terrified, bulging eyes. I ran breathless to the place on Leona Sapiehy where my father used to stay during his visits to

Lwów. It was an apartment of two or three rooms and a kitchen, located on the third floor of a sizable building. Leona Sapiehy itself was a big thoroughfare, traversing the city from east to west.

I told my father's friends, the two middle-aged couples occupying the place, what had happened to my dormitory, and they invited me to stay. They fed me and put up a cot for me in the kitchen. I had only the clothing I was wearing when I ran out of the dormitory. We were informed about the German attack on the Soviet radio, but a day or two later we lost contact with the outside world.

I didn't see the Russian army retreat, but I still retain the image of a tall Russian soldier running in the middle of the street, as if in a daze, all covered with blood. His terrified figure became for me a symbol of the Russian army in defeat, a giant gasping his last breath. From the window where I lived, I watched for hours the rearguard of the German army, flowing by like an unstoppable river of foot soldiers, horses, soldiers on bicycles, motorcycles, carts loaded with provisions, and field kitchens. That entire mass was on the march to conquer Mother Russia to the tune of such German favorites as "Rosamunde," "Bin ein Tyroler Bub / Hab immer frohen Mut," and "Oh-la-li, oh-la-la." Many of the men on this march were going to die, but in the process they would drag most of us with them into the grave. In the midst of the invasion, I continued to study my Greek verbs, as if I still had to take my aborted exams. I also spent some time in front of a mirror drawing my face. It was getting thinner each day, since we had very little to eat.

While the Germans were marching through, nobody dared to step out into the street. The march lasted about a week. The moment it was over, the city got a new Ukrainian administration and new Ukrainian police. Their dedication to the Nazi cause showed the moment they took over. They initiated their rule with a set of announcements and a massive pogrom.

The new rights of the Jews were enumerated in a series of proclamations in German, Ukrainian, and Polish. The Jews were forbidden to hold public or administrative jobs, they were forbidden to ride streetcars and trains, they were forbidden to change their places of residence, and they were to deliver all their valuables, including furs, to a place super-vised by the Germans and the local police.

Most Ukrainians greeted the Germans as their liberators. They must have thought that the Germans would let them have an independent state, but they were soon disabused of that notion. Western Ukraine be-came part of the General Government, which encompassed all of Gali-cia and most of Poland, while the western part of Poland was incorporated into the German Reich. But western Ukraine became a German ally just the same, and it was most loyal in the implacable war against the Jews. They took to this war with a dedication that was matched in brutality only by the troops from the Baltic countries and by the SS itself.

I was standing near the window from which I had watched the army pass when I saw the Ukrainian police entering our gates. When I men-tioned that to the two owners of the apartment, they took off as if on wings without saying a word. I don't know where they hid, but they did not ask me to come along. I realized that they wanted me to stay put so that the Ukrainians could find some prey. And thus I was waiting in the middle of the room, waiting to be picked up as the sacrificial lamb. There was no way to escape. The police had surrounded the house and set up guards on each floor. And where could I go? To the balcony? And then what? Jump from the third floor?

The First Pogrom

With a number of other Jews, I was taken to a barrack on Pełczyńska Street, which before the arrival of the Germans had been used by the Soviet army or the NKVD. Now it had become a slaughterhouse for the Gestapo. When we arrived, a thousand or more Jews were already sitting on the gravel and sand of a huge square that in the past might have served for military exercises or parades. Right away I felt that the place smelled of death.

First I was ordered to wash a military car. I was terrified when I saw small groups of men being led into a hangarlike structure from which

there came repeated shots. Among the men were Soviet officials, political commissars, and Polish intellectuals who had missed getting away in
time. At one point I thought that I saw them bring in the Polish poet,
theater critic, and translator Tadeusz Boy-Żeleński, whom I had first met
in the Writers' Club. However, later I was told that though he was killed
around the same time, it was not in the barracks on Pełczyńska.

I too had hoped to run away before the arrival of the Germans, when
we learned that the war had begun. I had gone to the house of a man I
had met through my father and who had worked for Wanda Wasilewska,
the Polish writer, but he was gone. The same morning I saw another
writer, Jerzy Putrament, with a small bundle in his hands, running to
what must have been a meeting point with Russian trucks. When I went
to one of these points, nobody was willing to take me. So I got stuck with
the Germans. This, as I said, was the fate of most Jewish writers and
artists who were not given the chance to flee.

I spent two days in the Pełczyńska barracks. There were one or two
thousand Jews pressed together in the middle of the big square and swel-
tering in the early July sun. While I was washing the car, I could hear repeated shots coming from the hangar. Near me several Germans were
having fun with a religious Jew. They asked him to do knee bends, to fall
to the ground, to say Jewish prayers, and to let down his pants. Then
they grabbed him by his beard and cut it off with big scissors. When he
began to bleed, they kicked him in the rear and ordered him to join the
crowd. I too got a kick in the pants and was ordered to join the crowd on
the ground.

Machine guns had been placed all around us on the roofs of the barracks, and pigeons were flying around them or ambulating in pairs on the
roofs. Oh, those pigeons! How I envied them! Why, I thought, should
pigeons be privileged to lead normal and thoughtless lives, while we had
to sit in the broiling sun, contemplating the precarious existence of man,
our bitter fate, and eventual death?

When night came, we were ordered to stretch out with our faces in
the gravel and sand. Soldiers were trampling over us with their heavy
boots, ordering us to bury our heads deep into the sand. From time to

time we heard the screams of people whose heads were hit with rifle butts or with clubs. The screams of the wounded were accompanied by the shouts of the Germans: *"Jude! Jude verrecke!* You and the Bolsheviks have executed thousands of Ukrainians in the Lwów jails and now you must pay the price for this crime."* The story that the Jews were responsible for the murder of thousands of Ukrainians was, as I learned later, a canard circulated by the Germans to incite the Ukrainian population against the Jews. While I was lying there, I thought that the night would never end, and I pressed my face deeper into the gravel every time I heard the screech of boots coming close to my head.

The next morning a group of important German officers arrived in cars followed by a dozen or so trucks. We were now sitting tight in the square, while the Germans began to pick out Jews in categories of a perfidious Nazi design. First they selected religious Jews with beards, drove them into the trucks, and took off. When the trucks returned, they picked out men wearing hats. Then they took away men in their thirties and forties. This process of selection and dispatch went on for several hours. The selection was done by officers of the highest rank—generals, colonels, majors of the army and the SS. By mid-afternoon only three or four hundred Jews remained in the square. We had to sit there in silence, but we could see the blood on some of our neighbors' swollen faces.

In the late afternoon there began a new selection: this time by profession. The Germans asked in turn for tailors, bakers, mechanics, and other métiers. Every time they called out the name of a specialty, I got up to join the given group, but I was sent back into the crowd with a kick in the pants because I had no document to prove my profession. Now they took away the specialists, and we never found out whether they were freed or taken away, like the previous groups, to a field outside of town to be shot. Most likely the earlier parties had dug ditches not only for themselves but also for the later arrivals. They were lined up in front of the ditches and fell into them after they were shot.

Toward the end of the day our crowd had thinned to about two hundred men. For this group the Germans had prepared a special treat. Soldiers armed with truncheons and clubs formed a huge gauntlet in the middle of the square, through which we had to run while being beaten from both sides. When someone was tripped or fell down, he was kicked to make him get up or splashed with water from hoses brought along for that purpose. When we were completely exhausted we were given the same bath, but we had to keep running, even if it was at a snail's pace.

Toward the evening the beasts had had their fill and they decided to let us go. But it was by no means a simple exit. We were rushed to the gates of the barracks, but instead of letting us out through the big gate, they opened a small door along the brick wall, so that in the rush to get out we tripped over each other and piled up in front of the wall. There, the unlucky ones who fell were hit again with rubber truncheons and bats.

Finally I got out. I was wearing a light summer jacket that I had bought for myself in the spring; now it was covered with blood, though not my own. I moved in a haze through the city, through the Aryan neighborhood full of promenading Ukrainians and Poles who looked at me wide-eyed, as though they were seeing an apparition. I stopped in front of an open window, and some good Poles offered me a glass of water.

This was the first bloody pogrom of the Lwów Jews, and those of us who went through it were the first authentic survivors in the war against the Jews.

I made it back to the house on Leona Sapiehy. The owners of the apartment who had run into hiding while I was picked up by the police were having their supper. They put down their spoons when I appeared in the doorway. They behaved like they had seen a ghost, because none of them could utter a word. But the women of the household led me to my cot and put me down to rest. They cared for me for several days until I recovered from the beatings and trauma.

I was not angry with the men for not letting me hide with them. After all, I was a mere intruder. They were lucky that they had a scapegoat to offer, for otherwise the Ukrainians would have turned the house upside down looking for Jews. The German Moloch had to be fed. After I moved out of that house, I lost track of the two couples. But in the fall of 1942, I ran into one of the men, the one who was friends with my fa-

ther. By then he was emaciated and his face bore the telltale signs of starvation, while I was just then doing fairly well. He looked at me as if he
did not believe I was still alive. I was sorry to see him in such miserable
shape, but somehow I could not muster up real pity.

Painting Signs

A fter my recovery I wondered how I was to go on. How was I to go
on living without money, family, or close friends? At this point the
Germans had not yet built the ghetto, but each day there were new re-
strictions on travel, on business, and on work. The Germans had introduced vouchers for food rations, but one could not survive on them. By
then one thing had become clear to me: I could not continue to stay on
in the house of my hosts. I realized that in order to survive I must get a
job, any job—with or without pay. The need to find a job became more
urgent when the Germans ordered compulsory labor for all Jewish men.
Anyone caught without a work paper (*Arbeitsausweis*) was bound to be arrested and shipped off to a camp. For easier identification, it was decreed
that the Jews must wear white armbands with a blue Star of David.

In the midst of these concerns I remembered that I had some friends,
namely the family of my Latin teacher, Walter Auerbach. It was Auerbach's sister, Dr. Groebel, who came to my rescue. As a doctor and a
member of an old Lwów family, she had a number of connections, one of
them with the owner of a large sign-painting company. When Dr.
Groebel asked me whether I knew how to paint signs, I told her that of
course I knew how; I had painted signs almost all my life, not to mention
the portraits of a marshal and of Soviet leaders. But my sign-painting job
turned out to be a fiasco, a complete flop. I had neither the skill nor the
speed of the professional sign painters, though in the process I learned a
few tricks of the trade. With thousands of apologies, the owner of the
company and friend of Dr. Groebel informed me that I was sacked. For
several weeks I walked the perilous streets of Lwów without a job.

The Ukrainian Museum

But the Auerbachs didn't give up. This time it was Ola who tried to help. She told me to see the curator of the National Museum at Lwów. The curator was a tall, elegant Ukrainian gentleman who received me warmly in his office. He greeted me in Ukrainian but switched right away to Polish. He told me that my job would be to copy the records of the museum holdings in preparation for a new catalog. In the meantime, he explained, the art treasures of the museum were all in storage. And, in fact, there was not a single painting hanging on the walls, and the heavy pieces of furniture standing in various rooms were all covered with white drapery. My working hours were to be from nine to two in the afternoon, and, of course, I was to work without pay. Then I received a piece of paper with a gold-embossed Ukrainian stamp stating that I was an employee of the museum. I was happy to have found such an easy job and an *Ausweis* with such an impressive stamp. After the brief reception, I got down to work. I completed the whole job in a few days, but I continued to go to the museum for about a month. The curator would show up about once a week. Otherwise I was the museum's only attendant. In the meantime the summer gave way to a chilly early October, and the place was getting colder each day, since nobody bothered to heat the empty building. After a while I reduced my services to about an hour a day, and on some days I didn't go to work at all, until finally I just quit. What speeded up my decision was an incident I experienced on the way to the job.

From the place where I lived on Leona Sapiehy there were about twenty elegant blocks inhabited by pure Aryans, mostly Poles. After covering several blocks, I made it a habit to roll up the sleeves of my summer jacket to conceal the symbol of my shame: the armband with the Star of David. I didn't mind it as much in the poorer neighborhoods as in the fancier quarters, where I thought it might offend the sensitivity of the *goyim*. But one day I was stopped by a Ukrainian policeman who asked me point blank what I had done with my armband. The excuse that I had unwittingly rolled up my sleeves did not persuade him, and he walked me to the nearest police station. It was an old, dilapidated building and there were only a few policemen on duty.

I was taken down to a basement with a concrete floor and walls of raw brick. For a while I was left alone, but then I was joined by a policewoman. She wore the dark blue uniform of the Ukrainian police and a pair of heavy boots, and she held a rubber truncheon in her hand. Without saying a word she hit me with it in the face and accompanied the blow with a kick. When she hit me again, I fell to the ground. Then she released her whole accumulated hatred of the Jews. She stamped on me with her boots, shouting, "You stinking kike, how dare you parade in our streets without your fucking armband? Just you wait, and your entire filthy tribe will be wiped out like rats." After a while I was hurting all over, though the insults and kicks were not the only source of my hurt. What bothered me even more was that the vengeful Ukrainian valkyrie looked exactly like a girl I had dated at the university, a good-looking girl with green eyes, pitch-black thick eyebrows, and somewhat high cheekbones inherited from her Cossack or Tatar ancestors. We had had a lovely time in Łyczakowski Park, where we spent many an evening talking and necking. It was the first time I'd had serious designs on a girl, and one evening I almost made it with her; we were prevented only by the wild cries of some drunken Russian soldiers who chased us all the way to the edge of the park. By late May, however, she was busy preparing for exams, and I never saw her again. The monster standing over me with the truncheon made me think that maybe I had never loved such a woman, a woman with pitch-black eyebrows and slightly protruding cheekbones. Maybe not only our loves but also our very existences were but illusions, the nightmares of a prostrate and beaten animal. Anyway, after about an hour in the dungeon they picked me up, gave me a bucket of water to wash my face, and let me go. And this was the coda to my job at the museum.

Baruch and the Twins

I still needed a job to earn some money. God knows, I never had enough to eat, and I suspected that my hosts on Leona Sapiehy helped themselves to some of my coupons. One day I ran into a friend named Baruch who had made a living under the Soviets painting portraits of the Soviet autocrats. An excellent painter, Baruch had been a certified member of the painters' guild because he was never short of commissions or cash. He told me that he was now painting license plates for military vehicles, and that he could use some help. Baruch worked in an abandoned factory on the edge of town that had become a dump and a repair shop for broken-down cars. In one of the rooms he had his workshop, together with his living quarters. In it he had set up a little stove, a worktable, and a cot. He also said that I could sleep at his place. I jumped at the opportunity, because staying with my hosts had become a physical and mental strain.

Our work would begin early in the morning and go on until late at night. We painted the plates for a pittance and could afford neither enough food nor wood for the stove. It was the middle of December 1941, and we were freezing at work as well as in our beds. A German soldier showed up every morning to pick up the plates, but we never received an *Ausweis* showing that we were employed by the German army. On one particularly cold day both of us decided that we had had enough. Several weeks later I saw Baruch in a column with concentration camp inmates. He had been caught in one of the minor raids and wound up in the Janowska camp near Lwów. Like the other men in the column he was haggard and in rags. He greeted me with a wave of the hand, like one who knew that he was on his last walk.

After the license plate job I could not go back to Leona Sapiehy. I explained my situation to Dr. Groebel and I asked her whether she would let me have a corner in her kitchen. I would set up a straw mat at night and remove it early in the morning. She promptly agreed to my request, and the kitchen became my home for the next few months.

I also found a new job. I volunteered with several house painters to paint two huge radio towers located in a suburb of Lwów. We were transported to the place by German soldiers who guarded the place during work. To get to the top we had to climb up to dizzying heights. From there we could see not only the neighboring orchards but also a garden of opulent cabbages right under our noses. The temptation to steal one of these cabbages was enormous, but the Jews working with me advised me to refrain. These cabbages, they joked, are expensive: a head of cabbage would cost me my head. Nearby there was also a transit camp for Russians deported to Germany for compulsory labor in the factories and on the German farms. The Germans hoped to fuel their military machine with an army of foreign workers, ill-paid and ill-fed.

The transit camp became my field of commercial operations. I began to move among the Russians, hawking accessories in exchange for food. In the city I bought up ribbons, earrings, bracelets, and other trifles and offered them to the Russian women, who had probably never seen such luxuries in their Russian stores. In exchange for these trinkets I got loaves of bread, chunks of butter, and, occasionally, preserves of jam. These I would take back to town in bundles and in bags to sell to the starved Jews. The job was not without risks, because Ukrainian guards watched everyone entering and leaving the camp.

Unfortunately, the business lasted only a few weeks, that is, as long as it took to paint the towers. However, in the camp I learned from one of the Russians that the Germans had suffered a major defeat outside of Moscow. This was exhilarating news, for it was the first time the Russians had stopped the advance of the German bulldozer. But at the same time the Germans had taken all of the Ukraine and were marching up to the Caucasus.

The loss of my business venture was also a blow to my morale, for it was the first time I had been able to make money for food. The winter of 1941–42 was in all respects a miserable time. I had been losing one job after another, and none of them, to boot, had paid any money. People were dying from hunger, and more and more men were being taken away to the camps. The newly organized Jewish police was particularly diligent in picking up people, for it had to deliver a steady supply of Jews for the camps. Moreover, it began to honor only work papers issued by the military—and I saw no way of finding a job with the army. In the hope of escaping the ever more frequent raids, I clung to my gold-embossed *Ausweis* from the National Museum, assuming that it would be recognized at least by the Ukrainian police. Having moved out of the apartment on Leona Sapiehy, I lost my right to the food rations allotted by the Germans to residents of each house. I had reason to believe that they went to my previous hosts. Thus I became almost a beggar in the house of the Auerbachs, who provided me every morning with a precious piece of bread. I was also unhappy to have invaded their home and to have taken over a corner of it for myself.

In the meantime I never stopped looking for a job—the only chance there was to survive. One day I stumbled into two boys, twins who had come from Warsaw and whose father had worked for a while with my father. They invited me to their house, which was simple but quite neat. They treated me to tea and introduced me to their charming young wives. In the course of our conversation the twins told me that they were working in a restaurant that catered to German officers and that they could use some help. They were peeling potatoes and chopping wood for the ovens.

The following day they introduced me to the chef, a middle-aged Pole with a long mustache and a permanent ironic smile. He had a somewhat rough manner, but underneath, as they say, he had a heart of gold. He seemed to have some sympathy for the Jews because for no reason at all from time to time he would mutter "leben und leben lassen" (live and let live). So I assumed that he wanted us to live. My impression was fortified by the fact that he hired me. For about a week I worked in the greatest harmony with the twins. We would take turns peeling potatoes, chopping the wood, and removing the garbage. Under no circumstances were we allowed into the dining hall, which was serving the officers of the Wehrmacht and the SS.

One day the twins informed the chef that the ax was too dull and that they practically had to split the logs with their bare hands. They gave him an ultimatum: "You give us a new ax, or we quit." The Pole laughed at the chutzpah of the two little Jews. "Well," he said, "if you cannot chop the wood with that ax, there is no work." So they quit.

The next morning I went to the chef and said, "You give me the ax and I'll go on cutting the wood." When the twins came back the next day and saw me hacking away at the logs with the dull ax, they became furious. They started to throw stones at me, shouting, "You dirty pig! You traitor! We gave you a job, we tried to help you, and now you take away our livelihood." I said to them. "Look, boys, you have each other, you have a beautiful apartment, and you have some money that you must have brought with you from Warsaw. In this city I am alone and if I give up this job, I starve. You see, I have no choice." They also had young wives in that nice apartment, though I was more jealous of the apartment than of the wives. I stayed on the job, but I could not forget the twins. Their shouts of "You dirty pig! You traitor!" rang in my ears for many days. I still hear it sometimes. Fear of starvation had taken hold of me and didn't let go.

I continued to chop the wood and peel the potatoes. In the fall of 1941 one could still move about without a work permit as long as one kept away from the Ukrainian police. New decrees against the Jews appeared almost every day and were displayed in three languages in all corners of the town. But the worst pain inflicted upon us from the beginning of the occupation was the rationing of food, especially of bread. The Polish chef who believed in *leben und leben lassen* did not pay us any money, but he rewarded us every day with a plate of soup and, occasionally, some leftover solid food. The stuff kept me alive but didn't still my hunger; in the midst of all that food, I felt even more hungry. I had to do something to fight the sensation. Being alone on the job, I began to slip two or three potatoes into my pants, at first furtively, and then with more daring and on a daily basis. I had tied the cuffs of my pants with string so that they ballooned at the bottom like bags. Jews of my age, both men and women, had begun to tuck their pants into their boots or shoes to keep warm or to keep the cuffs out of the mud. For me this style became essential to my business. I sold the potatoes to Piotr Rawicz's family. My venture into the potato trade did not raise any eyebrows; on the contrary, it received sympathy and support, especially from Piotr's mother, a cultured and friendly lady who would pay me more for the potatoes than they were worth. With this money I would buy the pretzels or potato latkes that were being sold on all corners of the Jewish neighborhood. The latkes did not taste anything like the real thing, for they were made, I suspected, with an admixture of sawdust or straw. I myself could not make use of the stolen potatoes because I didn't have access to a stove. Later, in the camp, people would fight for the peels of raw potatoes, but having eaten them, they always wound up in my *Totenblock* with dysentery.

After a while, I lost the job in the restaurant along with my business. The Germans took over management of the restaurant, and the good Pole whose slogan was *leben und leben lassen* got scared of losing his property for employing a Jew, even though this Jew was tucked away in the backyard peeling potatoes.

Meanwhile, a Ukrainian family had moved into Dr. Groebel's apartment, taking over most of the rooms. Recent arrivals from the countryside, they had enough respect for the doctor to let her keep her bedroom and the kitchen and to permit me to sleep on its floor, as long as I spread out my straw mat at night and removed it the first thing in the morning. The mother of that family was a cook in a German kitchen, and at one point she asked me to come by there after working hours. She made it clear that I must come in through the back staircase so nobody would see me. There she brought out a small pot of soup, which I gobbled up in a hurry on the staircase. This was a totally unexpected bonus, though it lasted only a few weeks. Yet I felt both lucky and ashamed when I daily encountered people swollen from hunger.

Dr. Hafner and the Judenrat

Having lost my job in the restaurant, I felt vulnerable, though I thought that I would be protected for a while from the *łapanki* (the street roundups) by the *Ausweis* from the Ukrainian Museum. There was also the nasty, nagging problem of getting food.

The Jewish police were getting busier and meaner every day. They could not arrest people with good working papers, and they were running out of unemployed men. I tried to avoid them as much as I did the Ukrainian police. Whenever I spotted them, I would run to the other end of the street or hide in a store or a gateway. Thus, I was always jittery and quick-footed. I had a hunch that my *Ausweis* from the Ukrainian Museum had become worthless. One day, as I was walking in the street, I was approached by a well-dressed gentleman who introduced himself as Dr. Hafner. He asked me my name and he said he had a paper for me. It carried my name, and it stated that I was an employee of the Lwów Judenrat. The rest of the data, my photograph and the German stamp, were to be filled in when I showed up for work. "Why do you give this to me?" I asked. "And who pointed me out to you?" "You are a Jewish poet, aren't you?" he said without answering my question, and he left.

A few days later I learned that a secret committee had been formed to save Jewish intellectuals. Most Jewish writers had failed to leave before the arrival of the Germans, and among them I was now to be saved, this time as an intellectual. In fact, I got not only a job, but also a coupon entitling me to a free lunch in the newly established Jewish soup kitchen. Through the kitchen I reestablished contact with some of the Jewish writers.

The Judenrat was located in a two-story building in the poorest section of town, near the old synagogue on Starotandetna. It was always packed with people. In addition to the staff, there were petitioners, beggars, policemen, and pleading women. Some asked for an assignment to an apartment, having been driven out of their homes; some asked for coupons to get food; some brought their silver and furs by order of the Germans or to bribe the Jewish police. But the major task of the Judenrat was to keep up the lists of the Jewish inhabitants and to provide the quotas of people for labor or for "resettling"—that is, for the camps. On the whole, this was a pointless procedure because the periodic *akcjas* (raids) and the *łapanki* vitiated the work of the scribes filling out those lists.

I liked my job because in fact it was not a job at all. When I showed up at the Judenrat to take up my duties, I was informed by the head of my section, a former teacher, that it would be enough if I came daily around nine in the morning "to show my face." I could see for myself that there was no space for me in that tiny room, where several people were bent over piles of handwritten papers. After a while I decided that it would be enough if I "showed my face" only every second or third day. Now I had a job, lots of time, and the right to a free meal a day. But I was still hungry and had to find a way to get food.

The Spring of 1942

It occurred to me that since Jewish children needed an education and all schools were closed, I should try my luck at tutoring. I began to look for work by knocking at the doors of families with school-aged children. During one of my errands I was picked up by the Jewish police. Forgetting about my new job, I produced the piece of paper from the Ukrainian Museum. The policeman who caught me grabbed me by the collar and said, "You come with us." I thought to myself, "That's it! This time I am cooked." I was taken to a cellar in which there were about two hundred Jews. Most of them were emaciated, worn out, and in rags, as if they had already gone through the camps. There was not a spark of hope in anyone's face. Suddenly I remembered Dr. Hafner's piece of paper and I showed it to the nearest policeman. He used a profanity and said something like, "You idiot, why didn't you show this to us right away?" He took me by the arm and led me most amicably to the door. It dawned on me that the Jewish police and I, an employee of the Judenrat, were comrades in arms. We worked for the same outfit, we were useful to the Germans, and, God willing, we might even survive the war.

After my brush with the Jewish police, I continued to look for a job that would help me stay alive. I knocked at the apartment of a doctor with two children, twins about ten years old. Their mother was an elegant and fairly young lady. She wanted me to teach the boys math, Latin, and English, but above all English. She explained to me that they were planning to emigrate to England. They were just waiting for the papers. The trouble with the new job was that I did not know English. But the boys were young and I had been to the university. I figured I would get myself a grammar book and learn the language while I taught it. I did find a grammar book, but unfortunately it did not give the pronunciation of the words. I began with the English nouns and taught my charges to say "a boy," "a man," "a woman," all of them pronounced according to Polish spelling ("ah boy," "ah mahn," "ah voman"). When I showed up for the next lesson, the lady invited me to her living room and asked me where I had learned my English. Shamefacedly, I confessed that I had hoped to learn it on the job. I was fired.

But I did not give up. After a while I became a tutor to a butcher's family. They had a fourteen- or fifteen-year-old boy, to whom I became quite attached. He was round and blond with a kind of innocent face and a permanent smile. He was forever stuck in the house because his parents would not let him out. He had no one to play with, and I became his playmate as well as his teacher. This family recommended me to two of their relatives, so that soon I was a tutor to three cousins, all of them sons of butchers. I asked to be paid in food, not money. At first I consumed three lunches a day, but as food in the ghetto became more and more scarce, the size of the lunches began to shrink. After two months I lost the job with the cousins; there was not enough food for an extra mouth. I asked them to let their sons join my first pupil without extra pay, but they refused, probably out of pride. The chubby boy was not very gifted, but he loved the lessons. English was our primary subject; I was trying to make up for the fiasco with my first pupils. By then I had all the books I needed to teach the language. Our favorite story was Oscar Wilde's "Little Prince." Later I also found the sonnets of Shakespeare, which I read with the help of the Polish translations by Jan Kasprowicz. Not far from the Judenrat was an empty lot overgrown with weeds and wild flowers. Here, in this wild meadow, I would walk about reading aloud the sonnets of the Bard and learning by heart (in Polish!) such lines as, "Tired with all these, for restful death I cry, / As to behold desert a beggar born." The original words I learned only years later, when I also I realized how much I had missed out by reading the poems in translation. I also read Polish poetry and several excellent Yiddish novels.

After some time I moved from the house of Dr. Groebel to the apartment house where my pupil's family lived. My new dwelling belonged to an elderly lady who lived with her maid in two rooms and a kitchen. I was not to stay in the house during the day, but in the evening they put up a cot for me in the kitchen. My young disciple had a sister of seventeen or eighteen with beautiful black eyes. While I was giving my lessons she never talked to me, probably because we were never alone, but after

I became her neighbor she came to visit me several times in the evenings. These visits cost us more discomfort than pleasure. For one thing, the old lady or her maid would peep from time to time into the kitchen to see what was going on, and for another, we were both bashful and tongue-tied. On such occasions I felt that because of the war I was doomed to die a virgin. But it was not to be. God was merciful.

The spring of 1942 was a period of relative calm, even though the *ła-panki* went on and people continued to disappear. There were no children in the streets, and wagons daily took corpses to the cemetery. From time to time I visited the soup kitchen, not for the watery soup it served, but to pick up some bread. There I also met some Jewish writers I did not know before. I valued especially my acquaintance with Rachmiel Green, a novelist, and his wife, a poet. In the ghetto he did the work of a horse. He had a small wagon in which he transported lumber, furniture, and old rags. I guess the Judenrat provided him with the work. From time to time I helped him pull the wagon. People would meet him and say, "Don't forget to write it all down, because later no one will believe us." I couldn't imagine when he could find the time or strength to write. While he was dragging the cart, he taught me some Yiddish songs, most of them to the words of Itsik Manger, the troubadour of modern Yiddish poetry. Then I lost track of him and never saw him or his wife again. They were taken to the Janowska camp, where they were shot.

Other people also began to disappear. One day I went to Piotr's house and they were all gone—he, his mother, and his wife, Rebecca. I surmised they all got away on Aryan documents. It was the first time I felt envious of people with good "Aryan faces" and the money to buy the right papers.

Another loss was the company of Imber. He used to come to Shudrikh's place, where the three of us talked politics and tried to foretell the course of the war and our own fate. Shudrikh had faith in the Red Army and believed in the imminent defeat of the Germans. After the great *akcja* he lost some of that faith. Imber hated the Soviets and the Red Army, and he loathed the Germans. To him both sides were the greatest calamity that had ever afflicted the Jews. The first tried to destroy them by wiping out their faith and traditions, while the latter were wiping out the people themselves. Despite his gloom, he still liked to listen to Yiddish poetry. Shudrikh had practically stopped writing, but I scribbled away, as if there were no war. Under the influence of Imber's dark musings, I wrote a poem that reflected my mood at that time.

Ligt a yung un kon nit shtarbn
mit a koyl in haldz,
epes ranglt zikh farakshnt
mit der koyl nokh alc.

S'iz dem yung's abisl lebn
vos vert zikh mit gevalt
un kon nit stam in mitn tog
oysgeyn in a vald

Nor grine grozn vern royt
az s'nogt dem yung a bin,
a gele bin in mitn haldz
nit aher, nit ahin.

A hirsh blaybt shteyn in mitn loyf,
farrayst dem kop un shrayt
antkegn cunter fun der zun
vos blutigt fun der wayt.

Vayse brezes, yunge kales,
di kep shoklen far shrek,
s'tut zey vey vos zey cufusns
ligt a yung un ekt.

Kumt der vint, der alter kabrn,
beymelekh culib,
nemt er sharn erd un grobn
farn yung a grib.

A lad lies and cannot die
with a bullet in his throat;
Something still struggles
Stubbornly with the bullet.

It is the lad's bit of life
that refuses to give up;
it cannot expire just so
at the forest's edge.

But green grasses grow red
when a bee sucks at the lad,
a yellow bee in the middle of the throat
that would not be budged.

A deer stops in the middle of his run,
raises the head and screams
against the scarlet of the sun
which bleeds from afar.

White birches, young brides,
shake their heads in fear;
It pains them that at their feet
lies a lad and dies.

Comes the wind, the old gravedigger,
and for the sake of the young birches
he begins to scrape the earth
and dig for the lad a grave.

One day Shudrikh told me that Shimmel, a Yiddish poet about his age, was dying. I decided to visit him. I remembered him as a man with a round, babyish face and a big mane of hair. I found his place in a dinky courtyard, where I had to go down into a basement that smelled of urine and garbage. Shimmel was lying on a cot, bloated from hunger. His face was puffy, his eyes half-closed, and his voice raspy and hushed. At first he did not recognize me, but then he asked me to read to him one of my poems. He was not quite pleased. He liked, he said, the sentiment, but not the feel of the poem. To show what he meant, he recited to me a few lines from one of his poems and then the beginning of a famous poem by Verlaine: "Les sanglots longs de violons / de l'automne, / bercent mon coeur d'une langueur / monotone." He liked, he said, the density of the rhymes and the rhythmic fluctuation of the vowels. For that reason, he said, he admired the poetry of the French and the Russian symbolists. Having uttered all that, he was visibly exhausted. He closed his eyes and waved me on, as if saying good-bye. A few days later I went to visit him again. His cot was empty, and a neighbor told me that his body had been taken away the previous night.

The Cookies

As the days went on I made some new friends. Actually, they were not friends but acquaintances. One met some people in the street or in the Judenrat, exchanged a few words, and called each other friends. Most relations were flimsy, because in the uncertainty of life nobody wanted to get too close. Food was scarce, and one was not disposed to share one's bread or drinks. There was some ersatz coffee around that tasted like swill, and we had only saccharine for sweetening. To my surprise, I discovered that some women were still baking cookies.

One such woman was Hana. I met her in the usual way, somewhere in the street, or perhaps it was her husband who invited me to their apartment for tea. He was a balding man of about forty, with heavy glasses and a slight stoop. He had a dour expression, perhaps because of a troubling ulcer or because of the miseries at his work. He had been a bookkeeper before the war, but now he was doing some kind of physical labor in a factory producing iron stoves. Hana was about ten years younger than her husband. She had straw-colored hair, sky-blue eyes, and a cheerful disposition. She also liked to sing. Her repertoire included Ukrainian, Polish, and Yiddish songs, all of a sentimental variety. Every Saturday evening I visited their apartment. Besides the house of my young student, this was the only place where I felt at home. After all, I had not had a home since my departure from Warsaw in October 1939. During my visits we had tea with Hana's baked cookies, and when night fell, we remained seated in the dark. All three of us shared in the singing, though Hana led the way. These were good moments in our hopeless existence.

Troubles with the Judenrat

Several days a week I would "go to work." The Judenrat operated very well without me. The building was always crowded and buzzing with rumors. The German army was still on the march, now in southern Russia and in the Caucasus. Some news would arrive about the liquidation of the Jews in the small towns, but it was all hearsay. Nobody could predict the coming storm.

One day I was asked to show up around nine in the evening for some extra work. They must have called up about twenty of us, all younger employees. We sat around for about two hours with a detachment of Jewish policemen, mostly middle-class Jews who had got their jobs for money or through connections. Among them were some decent men, but most of them were brutes or had become brutish with practice. By midnight, one of their captains arrived. "Gentlemen," he said in Polish, "we have before us a responsible and painful task. Tonight we must deliver to the Gestapo about fifty Jewish men. The Germans asked us, rather than the Ukrainians, to do the job. You know what happens when the Ukrainians invade Jewish homes. To bring in that many men we don't have enough Jewish policemen, and if we fail to do it, we, the Jewish police, will pay the price. You are members of the Judenrat, as are we. You must do it for the sake of our solidarity and to protect our people." Most of the men called up were stunned. Then and there I thought of tearing up my Judenrat *Ausweis*, but, of course, I did no such thing.

After the short briefing we split up into small groups, each led by a Jewish policeman. We fanned out into several streets. We started with the top floors, knocking at the doors. Frightened voices answered our knocking. Women dressed only in nightshirts opened the doors. In most homes there were no men. My companion, a youngish policeman, was very thorough; he looked into cupboards and toilets, knocked at the walls, and cursed the half-naked women. In one apartment he found a middle-aged man crouching behind the clothing in a closet. He dragged him out and led him downstairs. I used the opportunity to venture out on my own. I banged at several other doors but found no men. Suddenly I broke into an apartment with an old woman, a child, and a young couple in a bed. They must have been deaf to all the banging. The couple was terrified. "Why don't you crawl under the cover, you asshole?" I said to the man." Don't you hear what's going on?" I quickly left the premises and sneaked down to the courtyard to avoid the other policemen. I knew the outhouses of these Jewish courtyards quite well and hid in one until the end of the raid. Then I went home.

The following day I looked up Dr. Vogel, the husband of my former teacher who occupied a high position in the Judenrat. I told him that though I was grateful for my job, I had no intention of participating in the work of the Jewish police. He promised to look into the matter. I don't think the employees of the council were ever again asked to conduct a similar raid. I stayed with the Judenrat until the big *akcja* of July 1942.

July 1942

The *akcja* of July 1942 was a devastating affair. It was anticipated by rumors that had reached us from neighboring towns and shtetls. The Judenrat and the Jewish police had gotten wind of the latest movements of the Gestapo and were aware that a column of the SS was about to arrive. Unfortunately, they did not have the slightest intimation of the dimension of the forthcoming raid. When it was over it was clear that Jewish Lwów as we had known it had ceased to exist, and that this *akcja* was the beginning of our end. As we learned after the war, the "final solution" of the Jewish problem (the *Endlösung*) had been decided at the notorious Wannsee Conference at the beginning of the year.

Before the beginning of the *akcja*, I went to Auerbach's house hoping

to find him or his sister. But they were gone. The apartment was now occupied by a second Ukrainian family. The first family was that of the
woman who had given me soup outside her kitchen. I sneaked into Dr.
Groebel's office, where I found some cardboards and boxes. I tried to put
them together into a partition to be put behind one of the bookcases. But
the space was not deep enough and the partition fell apart. Then I tried
to climb up to a loft that was in the hallway of the apartment. But the
Ukrainian woman whose family had taken over the second half of the
apartment caught me climbing up the ladder to the loft. "Get out of here
right away," she said, "or I'll call the police." So I left. But instead of going
back to the Jewish quarter, I went to the Polish neighborhood where my
friend Frank Stiffel and his family had an apartment that I used to visit
during the Soviet occupation.

By now it was getting dark, and I expected the *akcja* to start at night
or the following morning. I tried to make myself invisible while I walked
through the alien and endless Aryan streets. Groups of Ukrainian policemen were marching toward the Jewish neighborhood. I withered and
shrank at the sight of them. I could feel Death breathing down my neck.

I went up to the third floor where the Stiffels lived, but a Polish gentleman answered the door and told me that the Stiffels did not live there
any longer. As I learned from Frank, when I met him again after the war,
his family had acquired passports as citizens of Guatemala and had
moved for a while to Warsaw. As it turned out, the passports did not do
them any good, and Frank wound up in Auschwitz.

Not knowing where to go, I went out into the courtyard, where I discovered a fire escape leading to the Stiffels' apartment. I took off my
shoes and climbed up to the balcony outside the apartment. There I
squeezed myself into a corner, leaning against the wall of the house. It
was getting cold, and at around three or four in the morning I fell asleep.
Disjointed thoughts and wisps of dreams were floating through my
head. I was back in the Jewish neighborhood, which was totally deserted. Many windows were open and I could see the curtains rustling
lightly in the breeze, but there was no one behind them. I moved closer
to one of the houses and tried to scream but could not utter a sound. Sud-

denly I woke up. A scraping noise was coming up from behind the stair-case. I opened my eyes and I saw a mouse rummaging in one of my shoes. It was getting light and I had to get away from there.

I went back to Auerbach's apartment, hoping to find him before he set out to work. Around seven in the morning he showed up. He hadn't slept in his apartment because of the anticipated raid. I assumed he had slept in the house of a Polish neighbor. I told him about my attempts to hide in his apartment and how I was chased out by the Ukrainian tenant. Auerbach worked for a German military outfit that provided him with protection from the raid. He told me to follow him on his way to work, but to keep at a distance so that if I were stopped by a policeman he would not get implicated. I followed him at some twenty paces through the looming terrors of the Aryan neighborhood. Next to his military post stood the wreck of an unfinished or bombed out house. He took me to a dark hole in the foundation of the ruin, which I crawled into. Inside it was pitch dark, but, as I soon discovered, there were two other men in that hole. One was the son of a worker in Auerbach's outfit and the other a more remote relative. These men had been lying on their backs since the day before. The father of the first man brought a small bundle of food each morning. He put it at the edge of the hole and the son crawled out and pulled it in. The other man got a daily package of food from a Polish woman who had been the maid at their household but was now his mistress. The deliveries were made in complete silence. To judge from the grunts and the smacking of lips, the two men enjoyed their parcels. They never asked me whether I was hungry. I didn't quite starve, because Auerbach brought me a small apple every day and the news that we should lie low. The *akcja* was in full swing.

After about a week the three of us crawled out of the hole into a courtyard in the middle of the ruin. It was a late Sunday evening. No-body could see us, because the courtyard was surrounded by a high wall and there were no houses nearby. The sun was setting, and when I hit the evening light and the fresh air I fainted. When I came to, I found myself in the arms of the two men and I saw their faces for the first time. We hugged each other and the three of us began to sing and to dance. After lying flat for a week and conversing in whispers, we were happy to be alive. We didn't know that the Jewish neighborhood had been practically wiped out. When it got dark we crawled back into our hole and stayed there for another two days until Auerbach came by and informed us that the *akcja* was over.

I left the hole and returned to the Jewish neighborhood. The day was brilliant, but the Jewish quarter looked like a cemetery. No one had yet ventured out. I started to look up some acquaintances. Most of the houses formerly occupied by Jews were empty, their inhabitants gone. My old landlady and her maid had disappeared. The family of the fat boy, my favorite pupil, had hidden in their butcher shop, where they were all shot. Deborah Vogel, her husband, and child were also shot in some store. The Jewish Council had ceased to exist. One of my former neighbors remained and treated me to tea and some fresh bread. Foolishly, I gobbled it up. After a while I got terrible stomach pains. Not knowing where to turn, I went to Hana's apartment. She had miraculously survived but her husband had been taken away. That evening my pains became so bad that I thought I would die. Hana called a doctor, and after a terrible diarrhea I was nursed back to life.

Hana

I looked around for new pupils, but there were none. The children had vanished, and my tutoring career was over. I had no money, and I did not know which of my friends had survived. Luckily I had Hana. She still had some money, and she was happy to share her food with me. At first I slept on a cot in her kitchen, but one morning I crawled into her bed. She acted as if she had been waiting for me. I was blind with excitement. Hana and I fell into each other's arms with considerable zest. I was finally cured of my virginity, which had been a source of embarrassment since I reached some maturity. My high school friends had been screwing their Polish maids at sixteen and seventeen, while I blushed whenever I got near a pretty girl. But the following night I had a feeling of unease: I thought there was a third party in our bed watching us make love. It was the shadow of Hana's husband. I dismissed the vision and in the morning

Hana tried to console me. "It is not for us," she said, "to judge who is to live and who is to die. We must take life as it comes. And aren't we a chosen people? Aren't we all destined to die?"

For two weeks Hana and I hardly ventured out into the streets. An uneasy calm had settled over the Jewish neighborhood, as if in expectation of a greater onslaught. It came in the form of a new decree.

The Construction of the Ghetto

T he Jews of Lwów were ordered to move into the oldest and filthiest part of the Jewish neighborhood within a few days. In no time, there was a new wooden fence surrounding the ghetto. It was about eight feet high and had one wide gate that was to be watched day and night by the Ukrainian and Jewish police and by some SS. No Jew was permitted to leave without a special permit, while the working brigades were to leave and return in a formation headed by an Aryan foreman. Hana's new place was at the very edge of the new ghetto. Her little brother and one of her younger sisters had taken up residence in a hovel not far from the old Jewish cemetery. That's where we moved. There was no reason to take along any furniture; there was no room for it in the new place. Many Jews had left better things behind. We brought along only some clothing and bedding.

Living together in one room became a real trial. There were five of us, including an infant girl whose parents were taken away and who became the charge of Hana and her siblings. I never learned how that infant had survived the *akcja*. As there were only two beds, I took again to sleeping on the floor. I felt like an interloper anyway. Hana and I would make love when the kids were out, but the whole thing lost its zest; it caused anxiety and became a strain.

My New Job

N ow that the Judenrat was gone, I had to find a new job, not for earnings, but for an *Ausweis*. There could be no safety from the police or a new *akcja* without a job in a military outfit or in a company working for

the army. But how was I to get a job without money or the right connections? But now again there occurred a miracle! Miracle was the name I
gave to my dumb luck, for without a belief in miracles, how was I to explain my survival amidst the relentless and devastating slaughter? What
right did I have to live in a sea teeming with sharks? Was I in any way better than my neighbors and brothers? In a world that was falling apart, the
belief in miracles was bound to replace the superannuated idea of hope.

I had run into my friend Norbert. He knew that the Judenrat was
gone and that I needed a job. He advised me to see the German officer
who headed LePeGa, the leather and valise factory that provided the
German army with luggage and pelts. Norbert's father was the bookkeeper in one of the branches of the factory, and Norbert had learned to
put together a valise. Norbert said, "Go to the German director and tell
him that you are a Jew from Danzig. He has a weak spot for German
Jews. Maybe he'll give you a job." I did as Norbert advised. I told the
German boss that I grew up in Danzig, that my parents were evacuated
to Poland, and that I had lost track of them. I spoke with conviction
using my best German. He looked at me with disbelief but he gave me
the job. At that time such a job was worth lots of money.

This branch of the factory employed about twenty Jews and four or
five Poles. The head of the branch was a Pole, a certain engineer, Czar-
necki. He never asked any questions, nor did he scold anyone. He
moved silently about the floor of the factory puffing on a pipe. I wrote a
little ditty about him comparing him to a Siamese cat. The real boss was
a Polish foreman, Borowski. He was a half-deranged sadist who was constantly on the move, telling everyone what to do. He didn't know the
business but he liked to shout, especially at the two German refugees, a
mother and daughter who shrank at the very sight of him, particularly
since they did not understand a word of Polish. There was also a Polish
errand boy of about fifteen or sixteen, whom Borowski treated as his
sidekick. From time to time I was assigned to him to transport valises or
pelts from our shop to the main factory. We had a cart that the two of us
were to pull, though in reality I did all the pulling. The nasty little fellow
walked behind the cart, urging me on and shouting obscenities.

However, the job in the factory was easy. One did not have to be a genius to bang together a valise. We had two clowns on our floor. One of them was Lulek, a fellow of about my own age. He was a valise maker by profession, and not a student like the other young Jews in our shop. He was witty and made us laugh with his clowning and jokes. I envied him, because in addition to his wit, he had a "good face": a short nose, blond hair, blue eyes, everything perfect to pass as a *goy*. He spoke a colloquial but decent Polish. In Lwów, even the uneducated Jews spoke a passable Polish, unlike the poor Jews of Warsaw and of the little shtetls, who spoke mostly Yiddish. The other clown was a Pole, Bolciu, who, like Lulek, was a professional valise maker. He was always in a good mood, and he made faces behind Borowski's back. When the latter was not around, he imitated his shouting. He was a simple fellow, raised in the streets of Lwów, but he treated us all with respect and even warmth. After the liquidation of the ghetto he saved Norbert's life.

Our Living Quarters. The Jewish Duchess

After a while the people working for LePeGa were ordered to move into one house. The move was supposed to be for our protection, so we wouldn't be bothered by the Jewish police, who were always on the lookout for people without a job. Yet from time to time, the police paid us a visit in search of intruders. In our room there were about ten or twelve people, men and women sharing four beds and several folding cots. At night, when they were put up, there was hardly any room for movement. Our worldly possessions were in a common cupboard, on chairs, and on ropes strung across the room. Bedsheets or blankets spread over the ropes provided the only partition between the men and the women. Outside there was a corridor leading to a common kitchen and a toilet. Because of the lack of space we spent most of our time in or on the beds. Occasionally we had some guests; they stayed a night and they were gone. They were people who had suddenly lost their jobs, mostly because the Germans had liquidated their outfits to obtain more fodder for the camps. But one night we got a visitor who came to stay.

He must have been in his late thirties, from our point of view an older gentleman. He was well dressed, but we had no idea what he was doing or where he was staying in the daytime. At night he came to sleep with his girlfriend, who worked in our outfit. She was in her twenties, a mysterious woman with green eyes and a feline, undulating walk. She hardly talked to any of us and carried herself like a Polish duchess. Rumor had it that she had been a nightclub singer or an actress. We didn't bother to ask her. The peculiar thing about her and her secretive boyfriend was the way they carried on.

Though we were crammed like herring in a single room, we never turned any visitor away. Nor did we much care who slept with whom. The only thing we worried about was typhus, which had spread through the ghetto like wildfire. Our room was miraculously spared, but Norbert and his sister, who lived in another apartment, came down with the disease. When I visited them, they were dripping with sweat and tossing in their beds like fish on dry sand. I was sure they would die, but they survived. Amidst all the misery and constant fear of the Germans, our duchess and her boyfriend carried on, as if they were living in some southern resort. They talked in whispers, held hands, cooed and smiled at each other, as if the rest of us did not exist. And we never saw them eat. There was something irritating and offensive about their hunger for each other, less easily tolerated since the man had no business coming night after night to our place. But we let them be. They did not make any noise, and the man would vanish early in the morning before the rest of us marched off to work. Then one night he did not show up. The duchess was sitting stiffly on her bed, glancing repeatedly at her watch. Then she put on her coat and walked outside into the cold November night. Up and down she paced in the long corridor. The next few days she didn't go to work. In the evening she was sitting on the bed waiting for her man to show up. Some of us tried to get some information about him from the Jewish police, but there was no trace of him. That people would suddenly disappear from the ghetto was, of course, nothing new, but our duchess was not ready to accept this fact. Then she too disappeared. After a few days we learned from the Jewish police that they found her in the basement of a neighboring house. She had poisoned herself with a cyanide pill.

How I Became a Forger

Toward the end of 1942, the Germans decided to thin out the ghetto again, leaving only those who worked for the army or war supply companies. The Jews working in such outfits were given white patches embroidered with the letter *W* for *Wehrmacht* (army) and *R* for *Rüstung* (supplies), each stamped with the black German eagle. The Jews who did not get the patches (and these included workers in some major military outfits) lost their right to exist. Some officers of the Gestapo must have received huge bribes both from Jews and from the German civilian bosses to keep certain outfits afloat. The patches were worn on the left side of the chest to insure visibility. The workers of LePeGa received a patch with the letter *W.*

Norbert had some friends who did not get the patch and were now in danger of immediate deportation. Norbert came to me in the evening before the *akcja.* "Look," he said, "four of my friends are in trouble and I hope we can save them. With your help! My sister Sophie will embroider the letters, but you must draw the stamp with the German eagle. I'll get you a pen and India ink. I know you can do it."

After a few hours, Norbert brought me four patches with the letter *W* embroidered by Sophie. I worked late into the night copying the stamps. The swastikas and the eagles came out looking like the real thing. I was embarking on a new career.

The Killing of a Jew

The following morning all working commandos were lined up in a big square. Several trucks packed with German soldiers and Ukrainian policemen were waiting at one end of the square, while officers of the SS with their dogs were walking up and down our lines, as at a military inspection. They looked through each line, pulling out the men and women without patches and sending them over to the side where the trucks stood. But then they decided that they could use some more people and started to pick out people with patches. This selection went on for about an hour and was a nerve-racking experience. Officers with whips in their hands and big dogs moved along the lines, looking us over from top to bottom and staring into our eyes. At one point I thought that they were picking out the tall men so I bent my knees to appear smaller, but then they picked out some smaller men so I made myself look taller. They also picked out some children, but the women would not let them go, so they let loose the dogs on the children, and the women ran over with their kids to the other side. But then something unusual took place.

A high-ranking SS man asked a tall and sturdily built Jew with a neatly trimmed beard to step out of the line. He took him over to a somewhat elevated area in the middle of the square. The two men were about the same height, and for a while they seemed to size each other up with some curiosity. Then the officer slapped the Jew in the face and began to insult him, as if he had a personal vendetta against him. But when he raised his whip to hit him, the Jew pulled the whip out of his hand and lashed the officer across the face. The officer was stunned and grabbed the Jew by the beard. As soon as he regained his balance, he whipped out his gun and shot the Jew in the head. The whole scene lasted just a few minutes but we were all mesmerized. The officer and his cohorts then rushed at our columns and with shouts of "Jude verrecke!" and "Schnell, schnell!" they began to chase us to the gates and out to work. On this day the selection was over. We marched out in silence, still stifled by fear but strengthened with pride, for there was a Jew, probably a simple worker, who had stood up for all of us to the German beast.

My Business

The following day, one of the recipients of my art showed up in my apartment. She was, like most of us, in her twenties. She had studied medicine, and I thought that she and Norbert were in love. She did not come to thank me; instead, she got straight to the point. "My parents and two of their friends are hidden in a cellar. They would be grateful and they will pay you if you would make *W* patches for them." I said, "I am new at this business, and I don't know what to charge; but I'll do it and take whatever you give me." That night I produced several patches. And so I became a professional forger.

At first I worked only on *W* and *R* patches, but after a while I branched out; I diversified. I started to forge whatever came along: working papers, Christian certificates of birth, travel documents. My customers provided the blanks, and I put in the signatures of priests, of city mayors and Polish officials, with either Polish or German stamps. I treated them all as equals. I was paid in German marks and sometimes in gold. The gold was in *świnki* (piglets), referring to French or English gold coins, or in *napoleonki* (napoleons). A single *świnka* was worth about fifty dollars and was fairly small; in fact, one could carry it in the palm of one's hand or, better, stitch it into one's pants or belt. As I later discovered, one could conceal a *świnka* for a while even under one's tongue. After a few weeks of work, my belt was lined up with a number of coins, while some were stuffed into my boots.

After the last bloody *akcjas*, the beggars and swollen people had disappeared from the streets. The ghetto came to resemble a "normal" concentration camp because the sick, the old, and the very young had all been taken away. A person could buy food at any time if he had money, and some people certainly had money, old money. Some of them tried to acquire Aryan documents or foreign visas. Most foreign visas acquired for big sums from corrupt Central American consulates turned out to be hoaxes, and their proprietors were picked up in no time by the Polish or Ukrainian police and sent to the camps.

The Count

My most distinguished customer was a Polish gentleman who worked as an inspector for the LePeGa company. He occasionally visited our branch, but he talked to none of the workers. Because of his elegance and air of remoteness, we called him, half-jokingly, *nasz hrabia* (our count), though there was a rumor that he was indeed of Polish nobility. His name was Lutosławski, and he invariably cut a fine figure with his fur-lined coat, silver cane, and Clark Gable moustache. One day he asked me to join him in the corridor of our outfit. He addressed me in a most amicable way, inquiring about my origins, my education, and how I was managing as a refugee in his beloved Lwów. He was a lover of Polish poetry, and for a while we chatted about our favorite poets and poems. But then he uttered in a whisper that he had some friends, highly educated and distinguished persons in need of help. I realized right away what he had in mind and I got scared. For after all, he might have been working for the Gestapo and had come to find me out. He assured me that he had the noblest intentions and that he wished to be my friend. God knows how he had learned of my trade. He urgently needed Aryan papers that would help several of his friends get away.

He brought me commissions four or five times. Each time we chatted for a while (mostly about the conditions in the ghetto), and each time he paid me on the spot. I became quite fond of him. But in April I left the ghetto, and I heard of him only after the war from my friend Norbert, who survived with the help of Bolciu after a dramatic escape from the Janowska camp. To my surprise and deepest sorrow, I learned that the count had been arrested by the Gestapo and shot. The great friend of the Jews was after all not a count but, like his forger and the people he tried to help, a Jew.

The Betrayal

I worked on my forgeries at night in a room occupied by about ten people, men and women. Some of them knew what I was doing, and I was afraid that one day one of them might betray me to the Germans or the Jewish police. I hoped that would not happen, for why would a Jew betray another Jew for helping to save Jewish lives? But betrayed I was, though in a tragic and completely unexpected way.

Lulek had a girlfriend, a slightly chubby and cheerful young girl named Rózia Feifer. She lived with her parents and a younger brother in the same building, but in a separate apartment. Before the war they had owned mills and an estate. They still must have had enough money to bribe the bosses of LePeGa to give them and their children jobs and a separate room. Every once in a while Rózia came to our room to spend part of the night with Lulek, in his bed. One night Rózia wound up in my bed. I don't know why or how this came about. Did she take a shine to me? Did she get wind that Lulek was hanging out with another girl?

Lulek did not mind the new arrangement. He remained as chipper and witty as ever. I felt I had to make up for his loss by taking him out every evening for dinner and by stuffing some money into his pocket. After all, I was getting richer each day, while he remained poor as a church mouse. Nor did he seem to mind when Rózia moved into our room, and when her parents began to invite me to their place for a late snack, as if I were a kind of son-in-law. This was somewhat embarrassing, since my relationship with the girl was nothing but a fling. Neither of us treated it as anything else. I liked her well enough. She liked to sing, to joke, and to giggle, and she liked the things I whispered to her in bed. She was smooth and cozy and full of caresses. But something was missing. Was it because Death was standing guard at our door? Or was it because we were all like casual passengers on a ride to our doom? Or was it, perhaps, because in the middle of lovemaking I kept thinking about our Jewish duchess, the mysterious creature with green eyes and a feline gait who had killed herself for love? Couldn't she have waited a while longer to come along with us for the ride?

One morning my things were gone and with them my friend Lulek. He had slipped out in the middle of the night with all my possessions. He took my shirt, my pants and my shoes, leaving me my *Ausweis* and the picture of my mother with my two sisters. He must have planned an escape from the ghetto for some time. As it turned out, he did indeed have another girlfriend, who hid him in the basement of her building while he was waiting for the right moment to get over to the Aryan side.

But he had miscalculated. A few days later the Jewish police were out on a house search and found him in his hiding place. They took him to the ghetto jail, and one of the policemen notified me that they had found him with my papers and money. The policeman knew that I had been robbed because his son worked in my valise factory. The Jewish police offered to give me back all the banknotes if I let them keep the gold. I thought this was generous of them, because they could have kept it all.

After Lulek's arrest, several of us went to see him. He was behind bars on the third floor of a ramshackle building that had been converted into a jail. Maintenance of the jail was a luxury for the ghetto because it was generally empty. The moment the Jewish police put someone in, the Germans or Ukrainians took them out and away. Lulek seemed cheerful. He waved to us through the window. "Hey, Edek," he shouted, "Here are your boots. To where I am going, I may as well be barefoot." He threw down the boots. He probably did not realize that some of my coins were hidden in the linings of the boots. But even if he had known, he could not have bribed the Jewish police, because after a raid they had to deliver a certain number of Jews "for the sands" (the generic term for a place of execution; in Lwów it referred to the Janowska camp). Listening to Lulek's joking, the girls cried and the boys swallowed their tears. The next day he was gone.

All this happened around December 1942 or January 1943. My work was still in demand, and I soon recovered some of my losses.

My First Attempt to Escape

Life in the ghetto was getting more perilous and more tense by the day. Restricted to the factory and to our rooms, we saw fewer and fewer of our friends. Hana had miraculously survived, but her sister and little brother were taken away. She had no steady job and was constantly in danger, though I learned that she now lived with some Jewish policeman. But this was no protection in a major raid. She showed up occasionally at my place, and I gave her money for herself and the little infant she took care of now as if it were her own child. Soon she moved and I lost track of her and the child. One evening I ran into Shudrikh. He hinted that he was going to join the partisans, for he kept saying, "We must save ourselves, we must fight! Future generations will not forgive us if we die without a fight." It was all very conspiratorial—not a word of when or where that fight was to be.

The idea of getting away also took hold of me with an iron grip. Several fellows at LePeGa and I started to speculate how we might get away to the partisans. We had learned through the grapevine that some Jews had formed their own partisan groups because the Polish and Ukrainian partisans did not accept Jews, or worse, that they robbed them and killed them on sight. The area around Lwów was not quite suitable for partisan activity, least of all for Jews. It did not have any large forests, and the population in the countryside was notoriously anti-Semitic. The situation was quite different in northeastern Poland, especially around Bia-łystok, an area known for its primeval forests. There the Jews were able to form their own fighting units. A few years ago I had a chance to visit the Bialowieża Forest, famous for its bison and wild boars. There I was also shown the graves of partisans executed by the Germans and their helpers. Even there the German army had organized deep forays into the forest, trying to wipe out the bands that were harassing their supply lines.

Several fellows in my factory began smuggling guns into the ghetto. We were getting the guns mostly from Italian officers through intermediaries. One such intermediary was Bolciu, the clowning Polish worker in our outfit. Thanks to him I acquired a beautiful Italian gun. We hid the guns wherever we could—in holes in the wall, in public bathrooms, in cushions and mattresses. We were searched at the gates of the ghetto, both when we left and when we returned from work. Once, the Ukrainians searched me while I carried a concealed gun in the linings of my boots, but they missed it.

Marching to and from work was getting more painful each day. We were searched at the gates for smuggled food, for coal, or for any item that would help us stay alive and were bloodily beaten if any such articles were found on our bodies. It was particularly painful when the beating was administered by the Jewish police, who, after all, were in the same boat as we were. Or did some of them think that they had a chance to survive? One had to marvel at the self-deception of these fellows. On top of it all we were teased and jeered at on our way to work. Hoodlums and ragamuffins smiled gleefully or whistled at our ragged column and called out to our good-looking girls to go to bed with them before it was too late. Respectable Polish or Ukrainian citizens passed us in silence; sometimes they gave us dirty looks, as if we were at fault for still being alive. To defy them and prove our bravado we sang a song that became our marching song and a kind of swan song of the ghetto.

Mamy wszy, nie mamy chleba,
Niech się dzieje wola nieba,
Pójdziem na Janowską spać,
Chuj ci w dupę, kurwa mać.

Chociaż smierć, jak wesz, nam bliska,
Przyjdzie kryska na Matyska,
Szwaba będą w mordę prać,
Chuj ci w dupę, kurwa mać.

Baw się, bracie, jedz i hulaj,
Jutro cię wykonńczy kula,
I przestaniesz się już bać,
Chuj ci w dupę, kurwa mać.

Gdy zawiozą cię na piaski,
Skończą się twe wszystkie troski,
Trzymaj fason i nie płacz,
Chuj ci w dupę, kurwa mać.

We got lice, we don't have bread,
God's will must be fulfilled,
We'll go to sleep on Janowska,
       Fuck yourself, you motherfucker.

Though death is close to you, like a louse,
There will come an end also to the Hun,
They will smash in his ugly mug,
     Fuck yourself, you motherfucker.

Play around, eat and make merry,
Tomorrow you'll be finished by a bullet
And you'll no longer be afraid,
     Fuck yourself, you motherfucker.

When they'll take you out to the sands
All your troubles will be over,
So chin up and do not cry,
     Fuck yourself, you motherfucker.

One day I got a signal to get ready to leave. I knew only one person in
the partisan group I was about to join. I thought I should take along some
money and a change of shirts, but my instructions were to come with a
gun; nothing was said about money or clothing. I found this somewhat
strange, but I thought I must trust the instructions coming from above.
The leaders knew best. When Rózia learned that I was going to leave,
she begged me to take her along. But my contact told me that no women
were permitted in our group. Then she persuaded me to take along her
brother, a boy of about sixteen. "You cannot save me, so save my
brother," she said. I could only marvel at her trust and naïveté.
     And so it happened that one evening in March we marched out of
the ghetto posing as a work team. We were led by a man who looked like
a Pole, since we could leave the ghetto only under the guidance of a gentile. We proceeded to a small train station located in a suburb of Lwów.
In a small wood near the station we had an information session in which
our leader instructed us to break up before entering the train, so that if
one of us got into trouble the others would not get involved. He mentioned the name of a small town in eastern Galicia where we were to get
off. There we would be met by an elderly man dressed as a peasant who

would lead us to our partisan unit. That was all. He wished us good luck and then he demanded to check our weapons. I was chagrined when he took away my Italian gun, giving me instead a revolver that looked like a toy gun. On top of it, I had developed a miserable toothache. We were told to take off our armbands with the Star of David and disperse in a ditch until the arrival of the train.

I was lying in the ditch near Rózia's little brother, who was shaking like a leaf, though he was still wearing his heavy winter coat. Before the arrival of the train, several passengers trotted up to the station. We were about to board the train when I thought I saw a Ukrainian woman who knew me as a Jew and I got scared. My comrades got into the train, but my little friend and I remained in the ditch. We stayed there for about an hour until it got dark, and then we made our way back to the ghetto. The Aryan streets were teeming with German soldiers and civilians. We walked with our heads down from fear of being recognized as Jews, and perhaps also out of shame for chickening out in the last moment. We proceeded to a remote section of the ghetto and climbed over the fence. The next day we went back to work as if nothing had happened. After all, nobody except Rózia and her parents knew of our failed attempt.

For several days I wondered whether I had made the right decision. But the recollection of my toothache, of the loss of my gun, and of the lackadaisical organization of the escape helped put my mind at ease.

A few days later I learned that a truck that was to take a number of Jews to the forest had been intercepted by the SS in one of the side streets of Lwów. The fifteen or so would-be partisans had been betrayed and were all killed in a short firefight. Among them was my friend Schudrikh. Thus I came to think that my decision not to board the train was not a mistake after all. Galicia was definitely not a place for a Jewish partisan movement.

Artek

After my aborted trip to the partisans I began to look for a new route of escape. At this point I ran into a young man by the name of

Artek. Actually I did not run into him; he came to me. I had seen him on
and off in the company of some shady characters, which led me to believe that he was a member of a ghetto-spawned Jewish underworld. He
was a few years younger than I. Although he was dark, he had an impec-
cably Aryan complexion, as well as some distinctly feminine traits. His
good looks must have helped him in his connections with the Aryan
side, for it was rumored that he smuggled cigarettes, vodka, and occasionally Italian guns into the ghetto. He was also a friend of some bosses
of the Jewish police, a crew that lived on extortions and bribes. He came
to me with the proposal that we run away together to Dniepropetrovsk,
the city located on the Dniepr River. He knew, he said, of a German military outfit that employed several Lwów Jews passing as Poles. He had
the address of the outfit and the names of two or three people on the job.
All we needed was a set of uniforms worn by the workers of *Organisation
Todt* and permits entitling us to travel from Lwów to Dniepropetrovsk. If
I provided the funds, he said, he would get us the original papers, which
I would copy. Of course, we also needed documents identifying us as
Poles. He was obviously aware of my business when he offered me the
opportunity to run away with him to the Ukraine, as long, of course, as I
took care of the papers and covered the travel expenses. He also insisted
on taking along his girlfriend, a young Russian Jew harking from somewhere in the eastern Ukraine. I could not object to that because she too
had a "good" Aryan face. Moreover, Artek claimed that she knew the ter-
rain. I readily went along with the plan. Dniepropetrovsk was nearer to
the front, and I figured I had money to last me at least half a year, that is,
until the Russian army took over the town.

There was no time to lose. It must have been obvious to everyone
that the Jews of Lwów, like the rest of Polish Jewry, were doomed. A
week or two later, Artek showed up with the necessary papers. He
brought several blanks and an original travel permit, which I copied with
the proper signatures, eagles, and Christian identities. A few days later I
bought a pair of German officer's riding pants and boots, after which I
acquired a green army jacket and a soldier's cap. My outfit was a mish-
mash of German services and ranks. However, people who worked for

the German army were wearing all kinds of uniforms. Thus dressed, with gold coins in my belt and my boots, I was ready to take the big leap.

I had hidden the uniform in the factory, and one evening, dressed up like a German, I showed myself to my friends. When Norbert's father saw me in that uniform getting ready to leave, he began to laugh, saying in Yiddish, "Take a look at this *meshuggener* (madman). Tomorrow he'll be dead." About a week later, Norbert and his father were taken away to the Janowska camp, and it was his father who died. Indeed, the entire ghetto was liquidated about a week after my departure. Everyone was taken to the Janowska camp, where they were murdered or sent off to Auschwitz. That was the end of centuries of Jewish life in the lovely, multinational, and multilingual city of Lwów.

Outside the factory I got into a *droshka* (horse and buggy) that took me to the Lwów railway station. There, Artek and his girlfriend were waiting for me. It was agreed that we would share the same compartment but that the two of them would sit at some distance from me. Artek bought the tickets, and we were off to Dniepropetrovsk.

On the train, Artek and his Russian moll got involved in a lively conversation with a group of young Poles who were, like us, on the way to a German outpost in Dnepropetrovsk. My two companions had, as I said, perfect Aryan faces, and they must have charmed the young Poles with their good looks and easy chatter. While this was going on, I pretended to sleep, hiding my face in my raincoat. But when I lifted my head, one of the Poles took a look at me and whispered to Artek, "This guy is a Jew." After a while, I noticed that he walked over to the next compartment, which was full of German soldiers. I was sure that he went to denounce me. I carried with me only a small valise. When the train slowed down in its approach to some minor provincial station, I threw out my valise and I jumped.

I spent the night under one of the freight trains parked some distance from the station. In the morning I stuck out my head to see whether a train was coming. A German soldier sitting beneath a nearby train was doing exactly the same. After a while he said to me, "Die Luft ist rein" (The coast is clear; we can get out). There was something gratifying and ironic about the help offered to me by a German soldier. On the next freight train I continued my trip to Dniepropetrovsk.

Dniepropetrovsk

With some trepidation I faced the vast alien city on the Dniepr. But I remembered that in addition to giving me the address of a "contact," a Polish Jew who could buy my gold coins and keep me in touch with the world, Artek had given me the address of a *melina*, a hiding place where I could stay for a few weeks without registering with the local police. At the *melina* I found Dora, a tall woman in her forties who lived alone. Her closest neighbor was a shoemaker, a man of about the same age whose outstanding features were his sunken cheeks and a considerable hump. At least once a week the two of them would get together for a little party. They drank, played the gramophone, danced, grabbed each other in the crotch, and carried on until late at night. Although the hunchback never exchanged a word with me, he filled me with repugnance and fear. I was sure that he was an informer.

Dora's outstanding trait was her greed. She demanded extra money for food almost every day, although I had paid her a hefty sum in advance. However, I was able to stay in her place for more than two weeks without registering with the police. The story I told her, and the one I was to repeat to other landladies throughout my stay in the east, was that I was on leave from a German semimilitary outfit, and that I was on my way home to Germany. Ostensibly, I understood only a few words of Russian. I counted on the general ignorance of my landladies as to who was who and what was going on in that war. Yet this was the first time I began to seriously study Russian, and I tried to read any Russian book I found in their homes. It was in Dora's place that I read *War and Peace* for the first time in the original. To my surprise, I also found there a book by Lunacharski, the red commissar of culture.

After two years in the ghetto, I experienced a curious sense of liberation. Nobody followed me or knew who I was. But living in hiding in an alien world exacted a psychological toll and had some terrifying moments. The most oppressing problem was the self-imposed silence. As a German on leave, I had to pretend that I hardly understood any Russian, and I found it a nuisance to depend mostly on gestures. My only possible interlocutor anyway was Dora, who cooked for me and brought me my daily food. There were no newspapers in the house, and I did not know what was going on at the front. I also had to be on the alert, hiding the Russian books whenever Dora came into my room. Knocking at the door was not part of her upbringing. Her nightly parties with the shoemaker were another source of strain. Although the house was located on the periphery of the town, I was afraid that the noise of their gramophone might attract the attention of neighbors and, ultimately, the police. Needless to say, neither Dora nor the hunchback gave a hoot whether I was able to sleep during their horseplay. On the contrary, they sometimes invited me to join them in their wild waltz. The hunchback would also utter some noises in reference to me. He was not sure, he would whisper to Dora, who I might be, and why I spent so much time in the house. While he said this, he pretended to be drunk, but at the same time he winked at me, as if letting me know that he knew I understood what he was saying. After one such party, Dora wanted me to go register with the police. I gave her some extra money, allegedly for food, and she shut up. But after about two weeks, I decided it was time to move on.

For the first time since my arrival in the city, I stepped out into the sunlight. I set out to look for my contact, the Polish Jew who I expected to change my coins for the local currency. When I got to his place, he asked me to leave and to meet him in the gate of a half-abandoned neighboring house. He was about ten years older than I, and he spoke with calm and self-assurance. He gave me rubles for my coins, and then, quite unexpectedly, he said, "Never come back to my place and if we happen to meet, do not let on that you know me." I had to give him credit for his caution: the man had a perfect Aryan face with a pair of God-given blue eyes, whereas my face was screaming Jewishness to the whole wide world. Then came the real blow. He told me that the "Dniepropetrowsk connection" was bankrupt, kaput. Some Poles had denounced a few Jews, and the Gestapo had been looking for Polish Jews all over the city and in the neighboring villages. "My advice to you," he concluded, "is to get out of this town as soon as you can. This will be better for you, as well as for the rest of us." At this point I realized that I was now completely alone, and that the front was still far away.

I went back to Dora's place, picked up the bundle with my extra shirt, my shaving equipment, a travel permit, and the instruments of my trade and proceeded to the railway station. I mounted the caboose of the first freight train that was going west.

For about two months I lived partly in freight trains and partly in small Ukrainian towns. I stayed longest of all in Dnieproderzhinsk. For nearly a month I managed to stay there in a *paselok* (suburb) with an elderly lady who never asked me to register with the police. In her little garden I spent a number of delightful hours with Pushkin and other Russian writers. It was my rule to stay away from houses in which there were men. This was not too hard to achieve, since most men had been drafted by the Soviets or deported by the Germans to work in the German factories and fields.

But even the best places were far from safe. One day I was looking out the window of a room I had rented in another *paselok* of Dnieproderzhinsk when I saw two Ukrainian policemen approaching the house. Without giving it a second thought, I jumped out the window (it was on the first floor). I stayed away from the house for several hours, walking around in a park and in some side streets; then I plucked up my courage and walked back to the house. I asked the landlady what the police had come for. She was not quite sure. She thought they were looking for work dodgers or some foreigners. Perhaps she did not want to tell me the whole truth. Nor did she say a word about my vanishing act. Afraid that the policemen might return, I picked up my bundle and went back to my former landlady.

One bright day I got in a line with German soldiers and officers to obtain army provisions handed out at major railway stations. After a while I became uneasy standing there with all those members of the Aryan race, particularly after one of them offered me a cigarette. So I took a walk on the railway tracks at some distance from the station, when a group of German gendarmes came along. It appeared that they were in charge of patrolling the tracks. They took me to a booth, checked my papers, and asked me why I was walking on the tracks. I explained that I became bored, as I had been waiting a long time for the next train. "Don't you know," they said, "that it's forbidden to walk on the tracks? Go back to the station." During this brief encounter I was sure that my number was up. But in the end I congratulated myself for my sangfroid and for the quality of my artwork. I went back to the station, got in line for my provisions, and proceeded back to Dniepropetrovsk.

I went directly to Dora. I wanted to prove to her that I was not some phony soldier or other suspicious character since I had come back loaded with German rations. Like a well-deserved trophy, she grabbed the sausages, the German bread, and the cigarettes and went over to the hunchback to show off the goodies, as if saying, "You see, you were wrong. Our tenant is really a German." But I did not remain at her place, nor in Dniepropetrovsk. The gifts were an investment for a possible future emergency. With the next freight train I moved back to my elderly landlady's home in Dnieproderzhinsk.

The Arrest

One day in late July I decided to get myself a haircut. It was the first time I ventured out to a barbershop. Waiting for my turn amidst a group of German soldiers, I was worried that a Ukrainian policeman might come in or that some local citizen might take me for a Jew. I had developed a theory (based admittedly on limited evidence) that for Germans it was not easy to spot a Polish Jew, whereas a Pole, Russian, or Ukrainian could smell one a mile away. Most of all I was afraid of young Poles. It was not so much a matter of looks, I theorized, as of smell—the consequence of having consumed from childhood the same potatoes and milk.

My first haircut in a public place went without a hitch. Encouraged by my success, I decided to visit the same barber several weeks later. It did not occur to me that I could cut my own hair, as I have been doing now for many years. Again the haircut went smoothly. However, on the way home I noticed a group of four men in front of a *droshka* in the middle of a big square. Two of the men sat in the carriage and two stood nearby. I looked at them and they returned my glance. Our eyes met, and I realized that they examined me with suspicion. I must have appeared nervous or I imagined that they took me for a Jew. Perhaps, I thought, it was the motley character of my uniform. The guys were civilians dressed in neatly pressed trousers, clean white shirts, and polished black shoes, not at all like the rest of the local crowd. And perhaps, I thought, they were Poles on an outing in town. As it turned out, I was wrong. For as I soon learned to my grief, three of them were Ukrainians and one was a Volksdeutsche; all four were agents of the Gestapo. Alarmed by their looks, I turned into the first street to the right where I accelerated my steps and began to run. The Gestapo men had noticed my maneuver, began to run after me, and opened fire. Their bullets missed me; I suppose they were trying to catch me alive. The street was a dead end, closed off by a fairly low brick wall. I jumped over the wall, but on the other side there was one of the characters pointing a gun in my face. The other three men caught up with us, grabbed me by the collar and arms, and started to drag me to the *droshka*. As we approached the carriage, I tore myself away and started to run toward an orchard across the square. But they were on top of me in no time. Now they beat me with their fists and the handles of their guns and threw me into the *droshka*.

The Interrogation

I was taken to a police station. I don't remember the details because I was woozy and shaken up. First I was taken to an important German officer, probably the head of the local Gestapo. He was slicing a melon and putting the juicy pieces delicately into his mouth. Near him stood a curvaceous young blonde, probably his Ukrainian mistress. He didn't ask me any questions but told the thugs who had arrested me to take me to another room, where I was interrogated by a Ukrainian gentleman with glasses, to all appearances an intellectual. He asked me whether I was a Jew, a partisan, or both. I told him that I was a student of classics, that I came from Lwów, and that I had been working for a German outfit. To test my story he asked me to recite some Greek poetry. I recited the beginning of *The Iliad* to prove to him that at least part of my story was true. He apparently quickly discarded the idea that I was a partisan, but he announced with some pleasure that I was a Jew. After these prelimi-naries, the thugs took me to a bigger room. They tore off my shirt, stretched me out face down on a table, tied my hands to a chair, and began to beat me with clubs and rubber truncheons. The beating seemed to go on interminably. At one point they hit me on the head, and I began to scream with all my might as if I had gone crazy. My screams might have confused them because they stopped. Anyway, they had plenty of time to call me back, and I knew that they were not done with me. After the beating they threw me into a cell where I could neither sit nor lie. My body was lacerated and bloody and I could only stand. Shaken and de-pressed, I wished I were dead. Then I recalled that I had concealed a razor blade in my trousers. I kept it during my travels to touch up my for-geries. The Gestapo had found my pen and India ink, but not the razor blade. Nor did they find the two gold coins that I managed to carry with me all the way to the camp. But in the meantime, I was going to cut my veins. I was tired, and cutting the veins with a dull razor blade was stren-uous work. My left wrist still bears the marks of my botched attempt. Feeling the first drops of blood and depressed from the effort, I stopped. I thought, "Why bother? Let the Gestapo finish the job."

The following day they brought me again to the big room. They asked for the names of my accomplices and the addresses where I had lived. I could not give them any names because the fact was that over the three months of my Ukrainian adventure I had met only one such "ac-complice," and I was certainly not going to betray him. But I listed the addresses where I had lived. As a result, they took me to several places around Dnieproderzhinsk and by train in a special compartment to Dne-propetrovsk. Dora and the hunchback got scared when they saw me in my wretched state and in the company of the police, but they could not tell them anything I had not told them myself.

A few days later I was put into another cell, this time one packed with people like a can of sardines. One morning all the inmates were taken out to work, except for me and a husky fellow who began to beat me the moment we were left alone. He called me a dirty Jew and beat me on and off during the long day. I realized that he was left in the cell for precisely that purpose. When the other inmates returned and noticed my black and blue marks, they said to the brute, "Why did you do that to him? Isn't he beaten up enough? Leave him alone or we will take care of you one of these days."

Igrenie

I expected to be shot any day, but the brutes must have had other business on their minds. About a week later they loaded most of the people from my cell into a truck and drove us under heavy guard to a camp called Igrenie. In Russian, *igra* means "play," but this place was not a playground; it was a killing ground.

There must have been about twenty thousand people, Ukrainians and Russians, sitting or sleeping on the bare ground. In the middle of a huge square stood an oblong brick building that had offices for the guards and a hall to which we were brought to sleep at night. It was a hot August, but the nights were cold. In jail they had let me keep my light summer shirt but had taken away my riding pants and my boots, replacing them with some old pants and a pair of ill-fitting shoes. I spent about a week in that building, sleeping on the cement floor. Near me there was a young Russian, Volodja, of about eighteen who lent me his fur-lined jacket as a cover. Even with him I exchanged but a few words. I tried to make myself invisible to the inmates as well as to the guards. The latter were not regular policemen or soldiers but *kapos*, that is, criminals and thugs picked out by the SS from among the inmates to maintain order in the camp. They moved around with truncheons, clubs, and whips like beasts of prey. One could judge the success of their work by the screams that from time to time pierced the air of the camp. One of them—I shall call him Ivan—was particularly brutal; he was plump and broad shouldered and moved like a gorilla flailing his arms. Suddenly and for no reason at all he would fall upon a prisoner with his whip and wouldn't let go until he drew blood.

There were supposedly no Jews in the camp. They had all been killed two years earlier, right after the invasion by the German army. But some Jews had apparently managed to survive. A few days after my arrival in the camp I was approached by a little man with suspiciously strong Jewish features. He bent over to me and whispered, "Amkhoo?" (a Jew?). I got awfully scared that the other inmates would see him talking to me and lump us together as Jews. I said to him in my broken Russian: "Get lost. I don't know you and I don't wish to know you." The next morning I saw him being carried out on a stretcher. Somebody must have denounced him to the *kapos* who probably killed him.

The same day we were all lined up on the huge square when the *kapos* started to march up and down, looking through the rows of men for another Jew. They must have gotten word that the man they had killed was not the only Jew. Standing in line with that mass of Russians, I found it hard to keep calm. When the *kapos* came to the place where I stood, I tried to hide behind the men standing in the front row. When the *kapos* looked to the right, I moved slightly to the left, and when they moved to the left, I switched slightly to the right so they wouldn't see my full face. This maneuver did not go undetected by my neighbors and it was my undoing. Also, my heart was beating so loudly that I was sure one could hear it a mile away. I knew right then and there that after the roll call my neighbors would betray me, not for some reward, but for sheer fun. Many of them were as mean and as brutal as their jailers.

The next morning I was called in to the head of the *kapos* for interrogation. He was a husky man with a scar across his chin and a booming voice. His main function in the camp was to dish out the chow at lunchtime, which he spilled from time to time in order to punish some innocent man. He too moved around the premises with a club shouting, "Galdyosh! Galdyosh!" (Noise! Noise!). Now he was stretched out in a chair like a pasha, with several bandits standing on both sides. One of them asked me in Russian, "Kak zovut?" (What's your name?). I confused the Russian with the Polish word *zawód* (profession), and I answered, "Ja maljar" (I'm a painter). They giggled as if they were amused by my mistake, yet they must have realized that I was not a Russian nor a Russian Jew. In shipping me off to the camp, the Germans apparently did not bother to send along my dossier or any instructions about what to do with me. They must have taken it for granted that I would be killed in that camp. But the one thing the bandits were sure of was that I was a Jew. To confirm that belief, and no doubt for some fun, they called in the camp doctor to check whether I was circumcised. In the meantime, Ivan, the overgrown gorilla, hit me with his whip, shouting, "Parshivyj zhid! Parshivyj zhid!" (Dirty kike!). Sure that this time I wouldn't get out of their clutches and that I had nothing to lose, I remained remarkably calm. "No, I'm not a zhid," I said. "I am a Catholic and a Polish student. If you don't believe me, call up the authorities in Lvov." They knew that I was putting on an act, but it didn't matter to me any more than to them. The doctor, of course, confirmed that I was a Jew.

At that point it was around twelve o'clock, and the head *kapo* announced that it was time for lunch. He said to his helpers, "Let him go now, but bring him back to me right after lunch." I figured he had postponed my execution until after lunch. Five minutes later—I didn't even have a chance to have a gulp of the chow (they served the same gruel each day)—there was a deafening siren throughout the camp. It sounded a general alarm, and in no time at all everyone was rushed to a freight train waiting for us outside the gate. We were being evacuated. The Soviet army was approaching and the Germans were on the run.

Arriving at Buchenwald

Now I found myself in a freight train with thousands of Russians. There must have been eighty to a hundred people in each car. We were on our way to Germany. Through the barbed wire windows I had the pleasure of seeing some German tanks running almost as fast as our train, westward toward the fatherland. We made brief stops in Odessa and in Lwów. I looked out with nostalgia at the city in which I had spent two relatively happy years and two of the most miserable years of my life. At one point I shouted in Polish to a passing railroad worker, "Hey, *panie,* throw me a piece of bread." He never even lifted his head. Packed like cattle, we traveled about two weeks. The guards didn't let us out, and we used buckets for toilets. We were sleeping on the floor and relieving ourselves in the buckets. Once a day the German and Russian guards distributed bread, a plate of soup, and a tin cup of water while the prisoners took out the buckets. On and off I was taunted and beaten up by young Russian hoodlums, who also stole some of my bread. An older man, a political prisoner or one arrested for no reason at all, asked the thugs to leave me alone. "What do you want of him?" he said. "He is not one of our people; he's a Pole, and he is obviously an innocent man, not a thief, like the rest of you guys." Didn't he realize that the thugs had their reasons? They were beating me up because they were anxious and bored and because they knew that I was a Jew.

However, the sport in which all of us took part during our trip was the delousing sessions. We would take off our pants and pick out and smother the lice. The biggest lice were saved for a race on the floor. The thugs made bets for pieces of bread and for the privilege of getting a share of my portion.

We arrived in Weimar early in the morning and had to climb several miles to get to the camp, which was located on top of a mountain. While we clambered up through the cobblestones of Goethe's town, I muttered to myself the exquisite lines of Goethe's "Wanderers Nachtlied." The last line, "Warte nur, balde ruhest du auch" (Wait, you too will soon find rest), acquired an ominous meaning during that march. Much later, during my stay in the camp, I learned that Goethe had composed his famous poem on top of Mount Ettersberg, precisely the mountain the Nazis had made infamous as the "KZ Buchenwald."

On the same day, we were rushed to the showers. At first I felt very uneasy in the crowd of so many uncircumcised men, and like a bashful maiden I tried to cover the telltale part of my body with my hands. But then I thought that since it takes a doctor to identify the scars of a circumcised member, I may as well stand up like a man. In the middle of the shower we were basically all alike. After this test, I never again hesitated to bathe in a public shower. After the shower we were shaved, deloused, and handed uniforms with white and blue stripes that looked like pajamas (in Polish they were called *pasiaki*) and wooden *sabots* (in German called *Holzschube* or *Klumpen*). It was the end of August 1943. After three and a half months of running around in the Ukraine like a hunted animal, I found my new "home," a place from which there was nowhere to run. I stayed there until the liberation on April 11, 1945.

The first man from our transport to die was Ivan, the *kapo* from Igrenie who had regaled me with his whip during my interrogation. The moment we came out of the showers, the Russians attacked him like maniacs. He tried to cover his head with his arms but fell under a hail of stones, and while he lay on the ground he was beaten with sticks and stamped on with dozens of wooden *Klumpen*. He died in a pool of blood, covering his head to the end with his arms. This scene of brutality and rage filled me with terror and disgust, though at the same time I experienced a deep pleasure at seeing that man die in an outburst of vengeance.

For some time our transport was to remain in a transit block (a block was a brick or wooden structure housing three hundred to five hundred men). Like all the men in my transport, I received a triangular red patch with the letter R (for "Russian") to wear on the left side of the chest. The following day they asked for someone who could paint signs for the new arrivals, mostly about keeping clean and maintaining order. I volunteered for the job; this was, after all, my old métier.

August Kohn

For two or three days I stood in a corner of the block painting the signs. People came by to watch and, as is customary, to help with advice. Then a big, handsome man stopped by to watch. He was wearing a red and black patch forming the Star of David. The red triangle stood for a "political" and the black for a Jew. The black triangles were also worn by the so-called "asocials." The big Jew was August Kohn. He was about thirty-five or forty years old and had been at Buchenwald since 1938. He was my new savior.

Throughout the war I had cheated death by luck and a bit of ingenuity. But as time went on, I began to believe that there was someone out there who wanted to keep me alive. Of course, I never dared to ask "who?" or "what for?" But look at the people who came to my rescue! First, there was Dr. Auerbach, then there was Dr. Hafner, then my friend Norbert, then the Lwów *batyar* (hoodlum) Artek, and now there stood before me this tall, good-looking man, August Kohn, savior or angel. I am sure that many survivors came to believe that their "good luck" was really the doing of some supernatural intervention. Perhaps the good Lord was making the point that every rule—in this case, the rule that all Polish Jews must die—had some exceptions. I found it somewhat amusing, of course, that my latest angel was a former leader of the Communist youth in the city of Leipzig.

August Kohn asked me where I had come from. I told him that I had come with the Russian transport, but that I was a Polish Jew. In the presence of Russians who did not understand a word, we got into a lengthy conversation in German. I told him about the Lwów ghetto, about my wanderings in the Ukraine, about our sudden departure from Igrenie, and about the fleeing German tanks. I impressed on him the idea that the Russians were winning the war. He, in turn, told me a few things about Buchenwald. I learned that during the late thirties the Nazis had murdered thousands of Jews there, that he was one of about two hundred Jewish survivors, and that he owed his life to the help of his German comrades. Though many of these had died, they were now in virtual command of the daily operation of the camp, having eliminated the rule of the German criminals who had been running the camp until 1941. I also learned that the remnants of the German Jews occupied a special block, block 22, which became my second, secret home during the twenty months of my stay in the camp. I would sneak in there only after dark so that nobody would see me associating with the Jews. But it was the Jews on that block who became my most intimate friends. I shared with them my hopes, secrets, and fears, and they kept up my spirits till the very end.

Toward the end of our talk I mentioned to August that I was unhappy with my Russian triangle, since I hardly spoke any Russian, and that I was afraid of being put into the same block with the criminals I came with from the Ukraine. "Let's see what we can do," said August. "In the meantime, don't be afraid. This is not your Russian kind of a camp." After a while he came back with a Polish triangle. "Put it on," he said. "Nobody is going to care whether you stay or die here as a Russian or a Pole." Thus I began my Buchenwald existence as a certified Pole.

A few days later I was summoned to the *Revier* (hospital). The doctors were German political prisoners, and, after a brief physical examination, one of them informed me that I was suffering from a severe heart condition. Who was I to argue with a German doctor? They assigned me to the so-called Strumpfstopferei, an outfit for mending socks and minor articles of clothing. It employed about a hundred men, invalids and cripples unfit for hard physical labor. The *kapo* of the *Arbeitskommando* was a big German called Wilhelm, a good friend of August Kohn, a former labor organizer from Hamburg, and a one-time member of the Reichstag. After a brief introduction he told me to go over to the nearby warehouse, where they gave me a pair of German boots, a decent pair of pants, and a warm, navy blue jacket. I wore this new outfit until the liberation of the camp. The change of clothes raised me automatically from the ranks of a pariah to the lower echelon of the camp elite. I realized that my new triangle, my phony sickness, my new set of clothes, and my fancy job were all the doings of my red angel, August Kohn.

The Story of Buchenwald

The history of Buchenwald was told to me by August Kohn, though I picked up a number of facts during my stay in the camp.

By the end of 1943, when I came to the camp, the everyday killings, floggings, and public hangings were largely things of the past. Dying still occurred on a massive scale, but there was no longer mass murder. The daily affairs of the camp were in the hands of the German political prisoners. The German Communists and Social Democrats had gained control of the camp around 1941, after a protracted struggle for power with the German criminals, who were identified by their green triangles. In addition to these two groups, the German inmates included homosexuals (marked by pink triangles), Bible students (the carriers of purple triangles), asocial elements (assorted "enemies" of the Reich marked by black triangles), and thousands of Jews. None of the minor German groups had any influence in the camp, and most Jews had been murdered before the outbreak of the German-Soviet war.

Many of the murders were committed by the German criminals in cahoots with the SS, and it was they who had converted the so-called labor camp into a slaughterhouse. They had a hand not only in the perpetration of the murders that were planned and coordinated by the SS, but also in the extortion of Jewish money, in the extraction of gold teeth, and in the theft of provisions destined for the camp. By the summer of 1941, the murders and lootings had reached such a vast scale that the Gestapo in Berlin decided to change the command of the camp. In addition to eliminating some second-grade officials, it removed the *Lagerführer*, Karl Koch, and his sadistic wife, Ilse Koch.

Indeed, it was the feats of the German gorgon Ilse that became a major part of the Buchenwald legend. People would recall how she used to ride around with a whip in her hand, trampling emaciated prisoners with her horse, and how she would watch the half-naked columns of men returning from the quarries and pick out inmates with interesting tattoos; these she would send over to Pathologie (pathology), where their skins were converted into lampshades for her tables. Among the other specialties of Pathologie were the injection of inmates with infectious diseases (above all, typhus, from which they never recovered) and the production of "Polynesian heads," that is, the shrinking of a human head to the size of a baseball.

The SS itself finally put an end to the rule of the criminals. Most of them were dispatched to *Aussenkommandos* (the outside branches of the camp), while others were finished with a shot in the neck to keep them from spreading bad rumors.

With the expansion of the war in the east, the new command of the camp must have decided to make better use of Buchenwald's human resources. Every ounce of sweat and blood was now to be squeezed for the military machine. The inmates were given new tasks: building huge subterranean tunnels, hangars for the newly invented rockets (as in Buchenwald's *Aussenkommando* "Dora"), and factories for the bombs and tanks. By 1943, the camp had gathered in citizens from all parts of Europe. The largest contingent was made up of Slavs (Poles, Czechs, Ukrainians, Russians, and Yugoslavs), after whom came the French, Spaniards, Italians, Albanians, and Greeks. In the summer of 1944 a transport of Danish policeman arrived, followed by another of Norwegian students. There were also some American fliers, although they did not stay long. The number of Jews in Buchenwald, who by 1943 counted only about two hundred, grew into the thousands by the middle of 1944, when the Germans abandoned Auschwitz and other camps in the east. The new arrivals, mostly Hungarian Jews, brought with them about fifty Jewish children from the ages of three to fifteen. The influx of so many forced the SS to open a second camp, the "Little Camp," which in no time became a cesspool of mud, squalor, and disease.

By the end of the war, Buchenwald counted over ninety thousand men. My own number was 28,851, and I had come to the camp only in the fall of 1943. The number of newcomers surpassed by at least tenfold the number of German inmates. But the internal organization of the camp remained until the end in the hands of the German political prisoners. They had won, as I said, the battle with the green triangles, who had for all practical purposes disappeared from the camp.

With the criminals gone, the SS had no choice but to hand over the everyday operation of the camp to the German "politicals." For one thing, they did not trust any foreigners; for another, they had been living with the German "politicals" for a number of years, and they knew that the politicals would run the camp like a well-oiled machine. After all, the concepts of order and obedience were equally shared by both sides. They also knew that the "reds" formed a highly organized group that could be counted on to maintain internal discipline and to deliver the military goods expected of them on time. In view of these facts, the politicals came to control all the important positions in the camp. They were the *kapos* of the working commandos and of the barracks (the blocks), and it was up to them to appoint their deputies, the so-called *Arbeitsälteste* and *Blockälteste*. Although these duties were generally assigned to members of the various ethnic groups, the German *kapos* tried to assign them to people of the left. In this, they did not always succeed, because the foreign inmates were a mixed and politically unreliable crowd, most of whom tried to conceal their pasts and political beliefs. Next in the hierarchy were the *Tischälteste* (the heads at the tables), the *Kaffeeträger* (the coffee carriers), the *Schreiber* (the scribes), and the *Calefactors* (the cleaners). The people working in the hospital and in Pathologie lived in a separate part of the camp, although they formed an influential secondary elite. All of these people could in one way or another affect one's life and one's very chances of survival.

Although the haphazard killings of prisoners by the SS and the criminals had ceased, there were still a number of ways to die. The more or less "normal" way to die was from hard work or from hunger, usually from a combination of the two. Work began after the roll call that was held at six in the morning. Most inmates were marched out in formation to the ammunition factories located outside the camp (the so-called *Werke* owned by Krupp, E. E. Farben, Siebel *Flugzeugwerke*, GmbH, and other companies), which would become frequent targets of air raids as the war went on. Other columns set out for the quarries (the *Erd- und Steinwerke*), located in pits a certain distance from the camp. Their work was to break up the rocks in the pits with picks and load the stones into lorries (trucks) that had to be wheeled back out. Since the number of lorries was limited, most stonecutters had to carry the heavy loads on their backs. In a matter of weeks, many of them lost their health and were carried back to the camp, half-dead or dead.

Hunger was as pervasive and pernicious as hard work. Food was served twice a day by the *Block-* or *Tischältester* at tables seating thirty to forty men. Around five-thirty in the morning, that is, before the roll call, one was given black coffee (a kind of slush) or a watery soup made with cabbage or turnip. A somewhat thicker soup (containing scraps of potatoes) was handed out at the work places at noon. The evening meal was served between seven and eight, depending on the duration of the roll call, which began at six P.M. but could go on for quite a while. Waiting for the end of the head count, our emaciated and worn-out bodies would shiver and shrivel in the fog that, like creeping clouds, forever enveloped the mountain with its long-forgotten name, Ettersberg. In the winter, the snow and frost would penetrate our pajamalike *pasiaki* all the way to the bone. Our only real meal was distributed in the evenings and on Sundays. It consisted of a thick soup made of turnip, cabbage, and unpeeled potatoes, a slice of bread (200 grams), and a sliver of margarine (10 grams). A trick one learned in fighting the persistent hunger was to divide the bread so that a piece of it would last until the next day's breakfast or lunch. This attempt to ration one's resources did not always succeed, for it went against the natural instinct to still the nagging hunger in one shot. Such lack of restraint caused one to be hungry throughout the next day and to try again with the next slice of bread. Men of stronger character managed to put some bread aside in their section of the cupboards, though this act created problems of its own; saved slices of bread tended to disappear. But woe to him who was caught stealing a piece of bread, because the first commandment of Buchenwald was "Thou shalt not steal!" The thief of a piece of bread could be smothered at night by his neighbors, wind up in a nasty place in the quarries, or be dispatched to an *Aussenkommando*. A more practical way of fighting hunger was to be on good terms with the *Block-* or *Tischältester* who handed out the soup. On Sundays, when the soup contained, in addition to the cabbage or turnip, some ground oats and scraps of meat (of uncertain provenance), a friendly hand might fish out from the depths of the kettle a heartier spoonful of soup or offer you *Nachschlag* (seconds).

Even more efficient was to have a friend who received parcels from home, although at a certain point the SS forbade the delivery of packages. However, I discovered that something valuable could be bartered for a piece of bread. The two gold coins I carried with me all the way from the ghetto saved me for a while from starvation.

The third major cause of death was disease. In effect, it was both quicker and more devastating than hunger or hard work. Several diseases were permanent afflictions of the camp. They included scarlet fever (known in camp as "the rose"), dysentery, pneumonia, and frostbite. People who came down with any one of these sicknesses barely had a chance of recovery. At best, they wound up in the camp's *Revier* for a few days, but they rarely left it on their own feet. During my twenty months in the camp, I got to know these diseases first hand, though they never affected my own health. As time went on, I learned that in addition to the aforementioned causes of death, there were other, sneakier ways of dispatching people to their maker.

New Faces and Old Friends

Most Russian prisoners who had come with me from Igrenie were sent out to *Aussenkommandos*. Only a small group of them remained in the camp. Among the younger ones, I recognized several who had beaten me up in the train. But now that August Kohn had given me the Polish triangle, I did not have to stay with them in a Russian block. Instead, I moved into a Polish block, number 21, in which I remained for two or three months. Here I should have felt perfectly comfortable—my language, my culture, the letter *P* on my triangle, all these should have permitted me to blend into the crowd. Yet I was not at ease. After my recent experience with the Russians in Igrenie and my years of mistrust and prejudice toward the Poles, I could not get rid of the fear that one day somebody might exclaim in the middle of a meal, "This guy is a Jew," or worse, that someone would betray me to the SS. This fear stayed with me for months, and I dreamed that one day, especially during the roll call, I would hear the yell: "Stankiewicz, zum Tor auftreten" (Stankiewicz, report to the gate). The gate was not only the location of the camp's Kommandantur, but was also a place from which no one summoned ever made it back to his block. But my fears were exaggerated. Buchenwald, as Kohn had said, was not "your Russian kind of camp." An inmate willing to betray another inmate could hardly have hoped to get away with it; any morning he could have been found dead in his bunk. Yet for several weeks I tried to keep to myself. This was relatively easy,

for the only time we could talk to each other was during supper or just
before nine P.M., before the lights in the block were turned off. But the
best time to talk and to make friends was during the long roll calls. Eventually, I got to know some people at precisely that time. Sunday was another good time to meet and make friends, provided one had established
some contact before.

In the meantime I realized how lucky I was to have gotten a job in
the Strumpfstopferei. Since most people in that commando were invalids or cripples, they were the first to be dismissed after the morning
roll call and to march off, half-limping, to work. We worked in a huge
cellar without windows, but it had lots of electric lights and was nicely
heated in the winter. Our *kapo*, Wilhelm, was seated at a desk at one end
of the cellar, from which he had a view of his two-hundred-plus charges
bent over their work. Wilhelm was a benevolent fellow but a stickler for
rules, mostly of his own invention. Talking during work was strictly forbidden, and at lunchtime we had to line up each day in the same order.
He himself dished out the coffee or the thin soup. The name of the outfit was somewhat misleading, for in reality we mended not only socks,
but also the jackets and pants discarded by recent arrivals before the
shower. The advantage of mending the heavier stuff was that in some of
their pockets were bits of tobacco, which I carefully wrapped up in a
piece of paper. These bits (the equivalent of no more than half a cigarette) I offered to a man on my block for a slice of bread. These remnants
of cigarettes were greatly appreciated, since neither tobacco nor liquor
were allowed in the camp. When word got out that I was trading in tobacco, several of my neighbors approached me for the stuff. But I reserved it for the man who had paid me with a slice of bread. His name
was Marian. He had broad shoulders, a ruddy complexion, very blue
eyes, and curly blond hair—all in all, a typical Polish peasant. His peas-
antlike appearance was reinforced by a somewhat crude, rustic speech,
harking back to eastern Poland. He had been in the camp for several
months and had made friends with a number of Poles, all of whom
looked and spoke like him. It turned out that he too was arrested somewhere in the Ukraine, though originally he had come from an area

around Lwów. There was something so simple and straightforward about the man that he won my complete confidence. I told him about the two gold coins which I had carried with me all the way from the ghetto and which were now sewn in the sleeves of my jacket. He sold them for two loaves of bread, which he delivered to me every second day in single slices. They supplemented my diet for several months.

On Sundays the camp did not go to work, and one Sunday Marian asked me to join him for a walk. The huge plaza where we used to line up for our roll calls was an ideal place for a long walk. Marian began telling me about his Polish wife, about the farm near Lwów where he used to raise chickens and pigs, and about his arrest in Kremenets Podolsk, in the eastern Ukraine. He was arrested almost by accident during a raid in a marketplace where he was trying to change money. It never occurred to the Gestapo that he was a Jew. The confession of his Jewishness came as a surprise to me, too, and I wondered whether my trust in him had something to do with a subliminal, atavistic bond. "But," added Marian, "I am so tired of being a goy; it's so hard to pretend forever that one is not himself." Then he added in the purest Galician Yiddish, "I would rather say daily my Jewish prayers than the three Hail Marys I utter to impress the goyim." Then he told me something else. "Do you know," he said, "that in one of the other Polish blocks there is another Lwów Jew parading as a Pole? His name is Artek and he too was arrested in Dniepropetrovsk. But he is a bad boy." I did not bother to inquire what he meant by "a bad boy," but I was all excited wondering whether "Artek" could be the same fellow I had lost on our trip to Dniepropetrovsk. The following Sunday I hurried to the other Polish block, block 25, to check on my hunch.

When I arrived at the block I asked for Artek, but I recognized him from a distance. He was as chipper as he was in Lwów, and, like me, he was wearing a warm jacket and civilian pants. He was all smiles as he talked to someone who, as I learned later, was his *Blockältester*. When he noticed me, he came toward me and whispered that he would see me outside the block. I realized that he did not want his neighbors to see us together.

Outside, he led me a certain distance away from the block. He did not ask me how I got to the camp, nor did he bother to tell me how and where he was arrested or what happened to his girl. The story he had to tell me was of a different kind. "Edek," he said, "do not ever come to see me in my block. I am doing pretty well here, and I don't want anyone to think that I have dealings with someone who looks like a Jew." When I protested that I am in the camp as a certified Pole, he said never mind, he would rather not be seen in my company. It was, he claimed, not only my face that must evoke suspicions, but my entire bearing, my walk, the way I hunch over in the cold; all these, he said, are the giveaway symptoms of a Jew. I took his harangue in stride. I thought that, despite his "good face," he was still running scared and that he was more terrified by the new surroundings than I. But maybe it was his way of asserting the superiority of a Lwów *batyar* over me, a budding intellectual. As time went on I never approached him again, especially after I had learned what Marian must have meant by saying that Artek was "a bad boy."

The *Blockälteste* of block 25 was a *Wasserpole* (a Pole from Silesia) who, as rumor had it, was involved in some shady dealings. He and his cronies had access to supplementary supplies and to tobacco, and they swaggered around with arrogance that must have been irksome not only to the other inmates but also to the Gestapo. Yet they got away with it, at least for a time; by the summer of 1944, however, the *Wasserpole* was suddenly replaced and we never heard of him again. In the meantime Artek had become his pal and the beneficiary of his largesse. Being well fed, Artek looked even more handsome and more feminine than he had looked in the ghetto. A smooth talker, he must have won the heart not only of the *Blockälteste*, but also of his pals. In other words, he became the whore of block 25. Although the Nazis had punished German homosexuals by putting them in the camp, they, as well as the inmates, looked through their fingers at the homosexuality that was rampant on the blocks. Nor was there any way of controlling what was going on in the bunks. Some people in power flaunted their gay relations quite openly, strutting around like roosters in the company of their boys.

Buchenwald had an official whorehouse, the Puff, but it did not do too well. The "girls" were brought in from a women's camp, but I never found out whether they were professional prostitutes or had been forced into the business by the Gestapo. The Puff was located behind a high wall at the outskirts of the camp, with the "girls" hidden away from the public eye. But patronizing the Puff was by no means a simple affair. An aspiring visitor had to submit his candidacy to the *kapo* of his block, and when his turn came up, his number was loudly announced on the intercom. In this way the whole camp was informed who was the next in line. Under these circumstances nobody cared to become the target of jokes and barbs, all the more because the political prisoners sharply condemned the whole setup as a cruelty perpetrated by the Nazis not only on the women but also on the mass of hungry, frozen, and mostly emaciated men. As a result, the Puff had only a short life (a year or two), and by the end of 1944 it had packed up, becoming, like so many things in the camp, a matter of the past.

In the meantime I was beginning to get acquainted with some men on my block. During a series of roll calls I found myself alongside a Pole (I'll call him Andrew) from the area of Poznan (Posen). He was well educated, tall, handsome, and talkative. He never told me what he was in for, but I gathered from his allusions and hints that he had worked for the Polish underground. He was a good patriot, which in his terms meant that he was both anti-German and anti-Russian. His feelings against Russia were strengthened by a fierce anti-Communism, which he told me he shared with his large, upper-class family, owners of grounds and estates. He spoke excellent German, having studied for a while in Göttingen or Berlin. He liked to tell me with a smile that he did not study too hard because he was repeatedly distracted by the German girls. He had a skimpy interest in books, but he had read almost everything published in both Polish and German concerning the Jews. I could not but admire his vast knowledge of the subject. He knew the names of old German-Jewish bankers, of Jewish astrologers who had deceived Polish kings, of the Jewish authors of the *Protocols of Zion*, and of the Jews who started the Russian Revolution. All these things he told me with an air of pseudoscholarly, cool detachment. But we remained good friends. I had the distinct impression that Andrew had never encountered a Jew in his life, and that he liked to impress me with all that knowledge. It certainly never occurred to him to whom he was talking. However, most of the time he talked about the Margaretas, Mimis, and Michaelas he had loved and had left. He told these stories with the same air of detachment as those about the nefarious machinations of the Jews. And then I lost him. The most nerve-racking thing about the camp was that one never knew when, where, or why some people suddenly disappeared.

Witek

A nother friend I made on the block was Witek. His first name was too long and outlandish for everyday use, so everyone knew him by his last name, Witek. We got acquainted during a roll call that I count as one of my most distressing experiences in the camp. It was in early December when the fog enveloping Buchenwald was exceptionally dense and the wind particularly mean. We were standing in formation, *Mützen ab* (caps off) and at attention, for more than an hour when the intercom suddenly blared out that there was going to be an execution. Gallows had been erected near the Kommandantur, and floodlights bathed the structure and the group of SS men around it in a white glare. Then they announced the names and numbers of the men to be hanged and their alleged crime: an attempt to escape. One could sense the unease running through our lines, because it was believed that the SS had by that time given up the practice of public hangings. They had so many ways of quietly doing away with men. I was glad that our column was at a considerable distance from the gallows. All I could see were the jerky spasms of the two bodies, followed by the thud of their dead weight. The execution lasted only a while, but it had a bad effect on my nerves. I muttered to Witek that I had seen a bunch of hanged men before, but seeing the actual hanging made me sick. "These are their last convulsions," Witek said. I did not quite understand what he meant, for the two men on the gallows had already been dead. "The last convulsions of the Nazis," he elaborated. "In the past they would have kept us standing on the Appelplatz at least three hours, while the execution itself would have dragged out for an hour. Now they seem to be in a hurry, as if they were no longer comfortable with the public spectacle." His remarks struck me as too optimistic, but they were heartwarming. On the way back to our block he asked me where I had seen the hanged men I had mentioned in the square. The question caused me some discomfort, for how could I tell him that the hanged men I referred to were the Jewish policemen strung up in the Lwów ghetto? I mumbled that I had witnessed such a scene somewhere in the Ukraine.

Our brief exchange on the Appelplatz was the beginning of a friendship that lasted throughout my stay in the camp, although it was full of bumps and uncomfortable moments.

Witek had been a student of law at the University of Wilno. He too had not finished his studies, but unlike Andrew, he was not distracted by women, but by leftist activities that had landed him in a Polish jail for a while. He was brought to Buchenwald from Auschwitz in 1942, in a transport of a hundred Poles, mostly intellectuals. Witek's mental life in the camp was filled with two obsessions: the course of the war and the future of Poland. He was convinced that the West would forever postpone the opening of a second front to permit both Germany and Russia to bleed to death. Hitler and Stalin were, according to him, military bumblers who had made a number of catastrophic mistakes and who would have been pushed aside long ago were it not for the brilliance of their generals. The German military command was smart, but it underestimated the three great assets of the Russians: their long and frigid winters, their endless reserves of men, and their capacity for suffering. These assets had enabled them to recoup and to deliver to the Germans a series of mortal blows, capped by the battles of Moscow, Stalingrad, and Kursk. Prewar Poland was, according to Witek, an economic and political morass that had to be swept clean, but the victory of the Red Army, he thought, would be a mixed blessing: it would create a new social order, but it would turn Poland into a subservient and semicolonial dependency. He was particularly wary of Stalin, whose terrorist methods had destroyed Russia's intelligentsia, impoverished its people, and torn apart the European socialist movement.

Over time, Witek introduced me to some of his friends. Most of them were teachers and lawyers; one was an officer; and the youngest, about ten years older than I, was a journalist and a writer. They were not all leftists. Several were old-fashioned democrats, a few were socialists, and two or three were orthodox Communists. These were the first Poles I had met since the beginning of the war who spoke with sympathy and compassion about the Jews whose destruction they had observed at close quarters during their own stay at Auschwitz. The greatest friend of the Jews was undoubtedly Witek, who recalled with warmth the Jews he had met during his studies in Wilno. At times it occurred to me that he suspected me of being a Jew, but if he did, he never hinted at it with a single word.

Witek and his friends liked to get together on Sundays. It was at such sessions that Witek would shine. As usual, he would hold forth on his favorite political themes, but he enlivened the meetings with aphorisms, ditties, anecdotes, and jokes, of which he seemed to have an endless supply, both in German and Polish. These he would recite slowly and with aplomb, accentuating for our benefit the relevant points. One of his German ditties stuck in my mind:

> Vorsicht ist die Mutter der Weisheit,
> Der Vater der Weisheit ist unbekannt.
> Davon geht hervor deutlich und klar,
> Dass selbst die Mutter der Weisheit
> Unvorsichtig war.

> Prudence is the mother of wisdom,
> the father of wisdom is unknown.
> From this it follows quite clearly
> that the mother of wisdom was herself
> rather imprudent.

For his light touch and wit Witek was greatly admired, but he was less of a hit with his political sermons. His friends on the right considered him a flawed patriot and a doctrinaire, while his friends on the left considered him a nationalist and a Marxist manqué. Both sides, however, agreed that he was emotionally shaky and slightly unhinged. Like a child, he threw temper tantrums whenever he thought that he was being crossed, betrayed, or otherwise let down. One time he grabbed me by the neck and started to choke me because I had failed to produce a birthday card with an appropriate little poem for one of the Poles he hoped to win over to the cause.

Our relationship took a critical turn when a new transport of Poles arrived in the camp. Despite the vacancies resulting from deaths and shipments to *Aussenkommandos*, the blocks were hardly capable of absorbing all the new men. In such cases, bunks normally designed for one had to accommodate two, sometimes three men. Witek was a friend of the *kapo* and was in no danger of losing his bunk, yet he would come over to my bunk after nine P.M. when the lights were turned off. For a while he maintained his usual banter with bits of gossip about his earlier life and the several women he had loved. All this was fine and good until one evening, when he reached for my private parts. I was both alarmed and annoyed. I was, of course, aware of what went on in the camp, but I took his attempt at my body as a personal insult and offense. I told him to get out of my bunk and stay away. When he would not budge, I repaired to the public toilet, where I spent several hours without closing an eye. The next night, when he showed up again in my bunk, I realized that I had a problem. I could not make a fuss and wake up the rest of the block, nor did I want to embarrass Witek and lose him together with my new Polish friends. It was again August Kohn who came to the rescue. "Why don't you move to another block?" he said. He recommended block 41, which was primarily German but had a number of foreigners. It was only a matter of waiting for a free bed. I jumped at the idea and after a few days moved to the new block. No one asked for an explanation about the move; similar transfers were common enough. Witek and I remained friends.

I met him again in the summer of 1960, when I returned to Poland for the first time after the war to attend an international conference. I ran into him by chance in the cafeteria of the hotel where I was staying. At first I did not recognize him because he had aged beyond his years (he was about fifty), in part because he had lost all his hair. We got to talking and he took me for a stroll to the Old Town (Stare miasto). The first thing he told me was that Poland was governed by a Polish-Jewish mafia that had put the country in a deep economic morass and political distress. I reminded him that in the camp he spoke rather well of the Jews. "But not about this Polish-Jewish gang," he said, "which was foisted on Poland by the Soviets to divert Polish hatred of the Russians to the traditional enmity toward the Jews." He had remained a maverick. He had been kicked out of the party and lost his job writing for a newspaper; he was earning a living by translating German technical books into Polish. His personal life was also a mess. His three or four marriages had ended in divorce, and he hardly knew the children he had fathered. Several years later I learned that he had died from something that started as an ordinary cold.

The Library

My transfer to block 41 was a cinch because, like everyone else in the camp, I had no earthly possessions. All I carried with me was a book I had borrowed from the Buchenwald library.

My discovery of the library was like a new lease on life. I was told about its existence by one of my friends in the Jewish block. The books were not in high demand; I was able to borrow several of them at a time and keep them under my pillow for weeks. The books were a reminder of a world that, though violated and bruised, was still one of beauty and wonder, and that, should we survive, we would still try to reclaim and enjoy. In reality, I was not thinking much of the future; the books were there and I wanted to read them, just as one wants to eat and to sleep.

The library was a treasure trove. It had books on philosophy, anthropology, history, and history of art, a number of German novels, and a few books in English. Most of them must have come to Buchenwald with the thousands of German Jews who had died before they had had a chance to read them there. But for whom did the Nazis preserve them? During my entire stay in the camp I hardly ever saw anyone reading a book. After the evening roll call most people were in a hurry to get back to their blocks, consume their meals, and get into their bunks. And since most of the books were in German, they were useless to most of the inmates. The existence of the library, like that of the Puff, seemed to be a joke of the Nazis on the mass of men who had neither the time, ability, nor desire to use them.

But when and where would I read the books? This question caused me some worry. Sunday was the only day free from work, but it was filled with a number of chores: mending clothes, going to the showers, cleaning the bunks, sweeping and washing the floors. It was also the day when the people from Pathology made their weekly inspection of the blocks. In its dread of typhus, the SS tried to stamp out any trace of lice in the camp. Everyone knew the slogan "Eine Laus—dein Tod" (A single louse—your death) by heart. The inspections meant above all an examination of the scalps, and though our hair was cropped short (sometimes with a tuft of hair left in the middle of the head), they tended to last more than an hour.

I decided that the best place to indulge in my reading was the Strumpfstopferei. The place was heated, had decent lighting, and I was tucked away in a corner, surrounded by a crowd of disabled men. The only problem was not getting caught in flagrante by the kapo. Wilhelm was a decent man but a stickler for rules, and I knew that reading on the job was a breach of the camp's work code and an insult to the kapo's authority. But I thought that I could get away with it, and indeed, I did, for a while. My solution was that of generations of schoolchildren bored with their classes: to hold the book one is reading under the table while pretending to listen to the teacher. So I marched off to work most days with a book tucked in the belt under my jacket.

The first books I borrowed were a mixed bag. I picked up Knut Hamsun's *Hunger*, hoping that it would somehow describe our daily condition. But the words about hunger were a far cry from the nagging sensation coming up from the depths of our guts, a craving we all shared but for which none of us had either the remedy or the right words.

I also got a book on the history of art, from which I learned about the wall paintings at Lascaux, the *Venus of Möllendorf*, steatopygia, and all the important Dutch painters. Among the various ideas advanced by the author, a German professor, was the claim that in the history of European art one can discern two distinct aesthetic strands: an earthly, sensual one typical of the south, and a lofty, spiritual one typical of the north (including Germany). Painters like El Greco and Michelangelo were exceptions. The lofty spiritualism of the Germans was something I got to know pretty well!

The German love of oppositions, the tendency to view all phenomena in the world as antagonistic forces striving toward a unity that could never be fully attained, struck me again when I picked up the works of two great German writers, Nietzsche's *Die Geburt der Tragödie* (The birth of tragedy) and Bachofen's *Mutterrecht und Urreligion* (Mother right and primitive religion). I took out the two books, thinking that they would take me back to Greece, the land of my high school infatuation. But neither of the books dealt with classical Greece or its arts. The true interests of the authors were the mythical origins of their subjects: Nietzsche sought the origin of tragedy in the chorus and dithyramb, whereas Bachofen argued that the patriarchy of Greece and of Rome had evolved from an older, more organic matriarchal state. The books filled my head with all kinds of anecdotes and ideas, but their deeper philosophical thrust was the struggle of such primordial and perennial forces as reason versus instinct, solar versus the lunar, Apollo versus Dionysus, and male versus female. It seemed to me even then that only German professors were capable of producing such high-flown and reductionist constructs of the mind. But my neighbor at the roll calls, Professor Ernout, assured me that similar flights of fancy were not a German monopoly. He informed me that the ideas of Bachofen had been adopted by such hard-nosed philosophers of history as the Marxists, while the cult of Dionysus had, by the end of the last century, been a craze with all kinds of mystics, poets, and scholars. "Notice," he added, "that the Germans have since Winkelmann and Goethe decided that they alone are the true heirs of spiritual and artistic Athens, whereas we, the Latins, are the heirs of a more primitive and pedestrian Rome."

In his youth Professor Ernout had studied with Georg Simmel and taught for years at Strasbourg University. Early one morning the Gestapo had rounded up the entire French faculty of the university and shipped it to Buchenwald and Auschwitz. We had spent many hours at the Appelplatz without exchanging a word, but one evening he asked me what I was reading. He had seen me with a book in my bunk before the lights were turned off. I had just sunk my teeth into Bachofen. When I learned that he was a professor of philosophy, I turned to him with all sorts of questions generated by my reading. He was a patient and enlightened man, and he advised me not to worry too much about the things I did not understand. It was obvious that he did not have much use for the vague and lofty ideas nurtured in the hothouse of German idealism. Under his tutelage I got into a book that stayed with me for some time, Lange's *History of Materialism*. But in the meantime there occurred certain events that, at least for some time, put an end to my studies.

Alfred, the "Kapo" of Block 41

Alfred, the *kapo* of block 41, was a slight man between thirty-five and forty. He was a puny and insignificant fellow with a singularly mean disposition. He was allegedly a Communist, but he felt a strong aversion to foreigners. Yet he was stuck with a block that had several Frenchmen, a number of Yugoslavs and Czechs, and, as far as I can recall, a single Pole—me. He treated us foreigners with undisguised contempt. He could enumerate the foibles of every major nationality of Europe, and he did so with gusto at dinnertime or during our march to the Appelplatz: the English were all pederasts; the French were weaklings and motherfuckers; the Italians were cowards; the Poles were dirty pigs; and the Russians were drunkards and thieves. On the way to the Appelplatz he urged us to move faster so we would be first to line up for the roll call. He saw to it that his block looked sharp. There was to be no slumping, yawning, or twitching, and little talking as long as the roll call was on. And he didn't like it if someone fell down or dropped dead during the count. But his true passion for order was reserved for the block itself. He had a mania for cleanliness, and together with the *Blockältester* made daily rounds to inspect the bunks. He would scream, shout, and throw fits when he found a blanket or a sheet improperly tucked in.

He took a special dislike to me from the moment I arrived in his block. I never acknowledged him with more than a nod of my head, to which he responded with something like a grin. I thought he must have decided at some point that I was a Jew, for why else would I leave a Polish block to be with a bunch of Germans? And why did I talk only to a Frenchman? I tried to ignore him as much as I could, but in the middle of the winter I got an ear infection and I received *Schonung* (a temporary work leave), which allowed me to remain in the block during the day. Now I could not escape him, and for hours we eyed each other in one of the block's two dining halls.

The swelling in my ear caused me great pain, and my head felt like a block of lead. I held it in both hands, as if to make sure it wouldn't fall off. At one point Alfred began regaling me with his deeper thoughts: Germany, he said, would have been a peaceful and great country were it not for the power of Jewish capital and the egotism of the Jews. This was recognized even before Hitler by Karl Marx. It was Marx who wrote that money was the jealous god of Israel, and that the creation of a civil order would be impossible without the liberation of society from the god Mammon and the elimination of the money-grubbing Jew. This harangue went on for some time and was intended exclusively for me, since I was the only person around.

When I recovered, I found myself on the list of people to be deported to an *Aussenkommando*. For me, this was the equivalent of a death sentence. My worst fear was of winding up with some of the Russians who had come with me from Dniepropetrovsk. The *Aussenkommandos* were also notorious for their brutal conditions and as places of no return.

Early in the morning I was marched out with a group of men to a remote section of the camp. In a block as large as a hangar we were arranged into columns of two hundred to three hundred men each. Among the *kapos* milling around us was Alfred, who in passing threw me a smug and sadistic glance.

While we waited for the trucks that would pick us up, I sent word through a German inmate to inform August or Wilhelm of my present plight. After a while, they both came running to the hangar. August remained at a certain distance, while Wilhelm talked to one of the head *kapos*, who pulled me out of the lines. This was indeed one of the dicier moments of my precarious existence.

My history with Alfred had a happy ending. At the beginning of 1944, the SS began to pick out younger German inmates for the Russian front. The color of the triangles no longer mattered. The German lines on the eastern front were crumbling in a number of places and were badly in need of bolstering with fresh contingents of men. In my *Schadenfreude* I was praying that Alfred be sent directly to the most exposed line of the front.

My "Kapo" Wilhelm

Back in the Strumpfstopferei, I felt an irresistible urge to thank Wilhelm for all he had done for me. Not only did he take me into an outfit made up of invalids and cripples, but he came running from the other end of the camp to save me, a young and insignificant Polish Jew, from the clutches of death. Or did he do it all to please his friend August? It was not for me to tell. Yet there was something unusual and decent about this *kapo*. A lion of a man with a mane of graying hair, a former fighter from the docks of Hamburg and the streets of Berlin, he was gentle and considerate with his men. He never pushed anyone around, he did not use obscenities, and he treated the weakest and littlest man under his command with respect. How was I to thank him? There were no flowers in the camp, and even if there had been, offering them to a *kapo* would have been a clumsy and absurd gesture. But soon I hit on an idea.

I would write him a poem, my first poem in German. Why not? I had
written poems in Polish and in Yiddish, so why not try my hand in German? The poem was to have nothing mawkish or personal in it, but
would refer to the courage and perseverance that kept Wilhelm going all
these years in the camp and to the hope of one day being set free. I found
a blank card, embellished it with a sketch of our infamous mountain, and
handed it to Wilhelm. At this point I remember only a few scraps of my
effort. It began:

> Wir sind die Partisanen
> Ohne Pferd und Schwert,
> Wir tragen keine Fahnen
> Und niemand von uns hört.

> Müd sind unsere Körper
> Doch munter ist unser Schritt,
> Wir tragen voll die Herzen
> Mit Hass, wie Dynamit.

> We are the partisans
> Without horse and sword,
> We do not carry any flags
> And no one hears about us.

> Tired are our bodies,
> Yet bold is our step,
> We carry our hearts loaded
> With hatred, like dynamite.

One of the following stanzas went something like this:

> Dann ist es aus mit dem Lager,
> Da sind wir frei zu Letzt,
> Es rauscht, es knallt, es hagelt
> SS-SS-SS.

Then it is over with the camp
And we are finally free,
It storms, thunders, and hails
SS-SS-SS.

Anyone who had spent some time in the camp would have recognized the first part of that stanza as alluding to the well-known Buchenwald song (composed by two Viennese Jews) that ended with the words: "O, Buchenwald, wir jammern nicht und klagen / Und was auch unsere Zukunft sei / Wir wollen trotzdem 'Ja' zum Leben sagen / Denn einmal kommt der Tag / Da sind wir frei" (Buchenwald, we do not wail and lament / Whatever our future / Despite everything we shall say "yes" to life / For one time comes the day / and we are free). One of the authors of the song was liberated rather early—but only by going up from the crematorium in smoke.

I had learned from August that Wilhelm was pleased with my poem. Encouraged by this success, I wrote several more German poems, but these I reserved for my friends in block 22.

In the meantime life returned to "normal": roll call at six in the morning, coffee or thin soup at twelve, roll call at six P.M. (for however long it took), turnip soup and a piece of bread in the evening, and lights out at nine. But now it was time to go back to my books and to the informed tutelage of my mentor from Strasbourg.

One day, right after the roll call, Professor Ernout introduced me to one of his university colleagues, a new arrival in the camp. It was Professor Unbegaun, a well-known Slavist who had been arrested with the other non-German members of the Strasbourg faculty. For some reason, he got to the camp several months later than Professor Ernout and left about a week after he came. In 1958, I had the opportunity to meet him again. By that time, I too was a Slavist. As I learned from Professor Unbegaun, he was released thanks to the intervention of Professor Vasmer, a distinguished German Slavist. I was delighted that after all these years he remembered our brief encounter in the camp, although when we had met my name could not have meant a thing to him. I asked him about the fate of my mentor, but he had lost all trace of him.

The book that was still lying under my pillow was Lange's *History of Materialism*, a volume as impressive for its weight as for its learning. It began with the philosophy of the Greeks and went on all the way to Kant. The title of the book was something of a misnomer because its true import was to prove the untenability of the materialist doctrine. The attempt to construct knowledge without the active role of an organizing mind appeared to Kant as chimerical as the positing of ideas without the sanction of experience. Kant was Lange's great hero, just as Lange was the hero of my mentor. As a result of my readings I, too, believed myself to be a Kantian, although the Buchenwald library had none of Kant's books. Nor have I ever finished reading Lange's book.

My Fall from Grace

It was precisely Lange's book that brought a change in my fortunes. During work, I kept the book I was reading on a small stool under the table. I would pull the stool close to me whenever there was a lull in the work, or when I knew that the *kapo* was out or was busy with things that did not pertain to the shop. I also trusted my neighbors; I was sure none of them would betray me about reading on the job. After all, I was as efficient as the rest of them. But accidents do happen. I must have kicked the little stool or shoved the book in such a way that it fell to the floor with a bang. The fall of the book marked my fall from grace. Wilhelm came running to our table, and when he realized what had happened, he turned red in the face and exploded with a chain of invectives. He called me an "intellektueller Spinner" (intellectual nut) and yelled that I undermined the discipline of his outfit and of the camp; he inveighed that my reading on the job was an insult to the hardworking invalids in his commando, and he added that I was an arrogant fool. In the end he announced that I was fired. Of all the harsh words, I felt most hurt by the label "intellectual nut," which I heard for the first time. It seemed to me that it contained not only the lowbrow distrust of the intellectual but also a dose of Red German anti-Semitism. As a man of the masses, Wilhelm did not have much use for people with a weakness for books. A Jew like August Kohn who had fought the Nazis in the streets and survived the early, most murderous years of the camp was clearly more to his liking than a little Polish Jew who had shown no respect for the inmates' hard-won and self-imposed rules. It also bothered me that he thought me an ingrate, though I never forgot all he had done for me since my arrival at the camp.

To my surprise I was only partly sacked from the Strumpfstopferei. I was assigned to the team of porters who remained under Wilhelm's command and whose job it was to transport the clothing shed by the new arrivals from the storehouse to the laundry and from the laundry, washed and mended, back to the storehouse. The distance between the two buildings was about half a mile. The clothing was placed on a wooden platform with straps, fastened with a rope, and carried on the back like a pile of bricks. The platform was about one and one-half meters high, but it could be twice that height when filled with clothing. The loads also varied in weight, usually weighing between twenty and thirty kilograms. My working companions were six or seven Russians, roughly my age. Among them there were two or three who had come with me from Dniepropetrovsk. I knew that working with them was bound to be trouble. It didn't take long for it to come.

I was put on the new job in March, when the snow was still fresh on the ground. The seven or eight of us moved in a single file like fantastic creatures with huge humps. If the snow was falling, we kept close together to maintain a straight line. As we trudged along under our yokes, it was not easy to talk; yet my companions amused themselves by reciting ribald *chastushki* (the *chastushka* is a short Russian poem made up of two contrastive couplets) or by competing in the use of profanities. These were either single obscene words that were declined, suffixed, truncated, or chanted in a number of colorful ways, or they were short phrases whose dominant theme were the sexual activities of your mother. Some of these phrases I had heard before, but never with the richness and ingenuity exhibited by my companions. All this kidding and chanting did not lighten our loads, but it certainly contributed to my knowledge of Russian, especially of *blatnaya muzyka* (thieves' cant or thieves' slang). For several weeks we worked without a hitch, except that

I always had to walk at the end of the line. This meant that when we arrived at our destination (i.e., at the gate of either of our two buildings), I was the last to discard my load. But the situation changed one day when we were told to take our loads not to the usual place, but to the car of a freight train standing not far from the warehouse. The train was generally guarded by an SS man, and whenever he happened to be around my companions acted up by jabbing me with their elbows, pushing me out of the way, or preventing me from dropping my load. I took the harassment in stride to avoid a disturbance. But I became far more concerned when they switched from physical annoyance to verbal abuse intended not only for me, but to attract the attention of the SS man. It consisted of the usual obscenities, though this time they included epithets with which Russian anti-Semites liked to regale the Jews. They called me *Khayim* (the Jewish name used as an offensive nickname for a Jew), *parshivyj zhid* (dirty Jew), and *obrezannyj* (circumcised). The insults did not bother me, but the fear that the guard might ask what the commotion was all about caused me considerable anxiety. It was helpful that the fellows did not know any German, but their pushing me and shouting was getting too noisy for comfort. One afternoon they became particularly obnoxious, obviously spoiling for a fight. To prevent this from happening, I withdrew from the train and started to walk back, briskly and without a load, to the Strumpfstopferei. But my companions were right behind me, like wolves that had had a whiff of their prey's blood. In the middle of our usual path I decided to stand my ground. I let loose with a string of Russian invectives that I never knew I had in me. The gang became quite mad when I called them *ur'ki* and *shpana* (the slang words for Russian criminals), and when I reminded two of them that they had stolen my bread during our voyage from Dniepropetrovsk. At this, the smaller of the two guys punched me in the face, giving me a bloody nose. The frontal attack was followed by an even more powerful blow to my ears from the bigger guy who was standing behind me. That really hurt, because throughout my stay in the camp I had had trouble with my ears (no doubt as a result of the treatment I had received from the Gestapo in Dnieproderzhinsk). Without thinking of what I was doing, I swung around and hit the big guy with all my might with the wooden platform. I must have shocked and disoriented him with my blow, because for an instant he stood there, eyes glazed and mouth open. But it did not take me long to realize that if I didn't get away in a hurry, these fellows would beat me to a pulp. There now remained about two hundred meters to the Strumpfstopferei. I took off like the devil with a bloody nose, the empty platform in my hand and several thugs at my heels. But I made it down to Wilhelm's basement, leaving my pursuers at the door. When Wilhelm learned what had happened, he took me outside and delivered a little speech that I translated to the thugs in my imperfect Russian. "In my outfit," he said, "I will not tolerate any fights. Anyone who is caught in a fight will be kicked out of this place, and I shall personally see to it that he is sent to the quarries or to an *Aussenkommando*. The rule of criminals is over in this camp, and we will not permit it to come back; nor shall we let innocent people die at the hands of fellow inmates; we leave this job to the SS. Now get back to work!"

After that, no further incidents occurred on the job. The Russians stopped teasing and pushing me around, and I tried to keep a respectable distance from them during work and at the midday break for lunch. But I watched my step, fearing that at any time they might try to show me who was boss. The only way to find safety was to leave them, along with the deceptive safety of the Strumpfstopferei.

Block 22

My fight with the Russians reminded me that immersion in a crowd of about sixty thousand men was no guarantee that I would get out of the camp alive. The German defenses were crumbling on several fronts, but the end of the war was by no means in sight. No amount of camouflage or good luck could wipe the stigma of Jewishness from my face, and my red triangle with the letter P was hardly a shield from the poisonous arrows of prejudice and hatred. But I was not about to give in to my melancholy mood. After three years of fighting an obstinate, almost personal war with the Nazi beast, I was not going to be defeated by a couple of troglodyte criminals. To lift my spirits I compared my lot with that of the two hundred or so German Jews who had been kept isolated from the rest of the camp in block 22. They had been hounded and beaten more than all the other prisoners put together, yet I never heard them utter a word of complaint. After years of unspeakable misery and pain, they were holding out like shipwrecks in a stormy and shark-infested sea. And thus it was that in block 22 I sought and found solace and some of my most reliable friends. In their company I could afford to let down my guard and shake off my obsessive persecutional angst.

I would sneak into the Jewish block nearly every second Sunday after dark, so as not to be seen associating with the Jews. Most of the residents of that block were middle-class and middle-aged men. August Kohn was probably the youngest of all. The other young men had been liquidated long ago by the SS, while most of the older ones had died from exhaustion or disease. The remainder owed their survival to luck, to special skills, or to the work they were performing in the camp. Several were raising animals on a secret experimental farm, several were noted engineers, a few were psychiatrists working for the SS, several were tailors, and two or three were doctors. It is to them that I ran whenever I got scared or depressed, and they never failed to receive me with open arms. But as I got to know them somewhat better, I realized how much they differed from the Jews I had known in my childhood and, later, as a refugee in Lwów.

It was not a matter of education. It is true that many Polish Jews were illiterate and that some hardly spoke any Polish. On the other hand, most of them had attended a *cheder* (the elementary religious school) where they had learned some Hebrew and conversed in Yiddish. Even the assimilated Polish Jews had heard about (or had in their own families) some famous Jewish rabbi, had encountered Hasidim, and had been aware of a thriving, if estranged, Jewish culture. The Polish state that had emerged after World War I was both too young and too nationalistic to allow the Polish Jew to feel that he was a part of that land. The anti-semitism of the Nazis was but an extreme, depraved variety of the slurs and hurts he had to bear many days of his life. The situation was com-

pletely different for the German Jews. Most of them knew only one culture: German. Even the simplest German Jews were familiar with
Beethoven and Goethe and had learned to recite a ballad by Schiller or a
poem by Heine. Their fathers and grandfathers had fought for the kaiser
and had won iron crosses that were rusting in their abandoned attics.
The German Jews had lost not only their families and possessions, but
also a fatherland, and with it, their sense of identity. What had hit them
was to their mind not a man-made, brutal, political force, but a cata-
clysmic event, something like an earthquake. Gone, therefore, was not
only the pride of the German Jew, who had looked down with mild and
amused contempt upon the uneducated *Ostjude* (Eastern Jew) but also his
very will to live. Hence the sense of resignation, a nearly catatonic apa-
thy that had struck me at the first as heroic detachment.

I felt that my visits to the Jewish block had somewhat stirred things
up. My friends were particularly interested in my stories about the
ghetto. They listened with fascination to accounts of our purchase of
guns, the Warsaw uprising, the partisans in the forests, and my escape
from the ghetto. I also tried to amuse them with a few German poems I
had written especially for them. These were mostly light verses in an upbeat rhythm or musings about the passing of things. In one poem I wrote
about the birds that never alighted in the camp, in another about a city
without mice or cats, and about dogs whose only use was to tear into the
flesh of men. Besides August, I developed a fondness for one of the tailors, named Kurt, a native of Breslau. Before the war he had been a pub-
lisher and a printer. After one of my visits he asked me to lend him my
German poems. Several months later he surprised me with a magnificent
gift: all of my twenty or so poems were printed by hand in the tiniest
script and on the thinnest paper in a booklet you could fit in the palm of
your hand. My friends celebrated the gift with an extra cup of swill especially prepared for the occasion. I asked August to hide it for me in his
outfit (he was tending experimental pigs) because I was afraid to keep it
in my block.

But the gloom in the Jewish block was not lifted. One day the SS
murdered one of the psychiatrists who had often been seen in their com-

pany. He was a round-bellied gentleman with a goatee, who walked around with a silver cane in his hand. His death came as a shock to all who had known him, for it was assumed that he had enjoyed special privileges because of his international reputation and because he had cured one of the SS bigwigs. Soon after, a doctor engaged in the Nazi experiments committed suicide. He must have acquired his arsenic or other poison right there on the job. And then came the most terrible shock of all: my beloved Kurt, the admirer and printer of my poems, hanged himself in the public toilet of the block.

The Nazis hounded the Jewish block to the very end. With the approach of the American army, the SS had decided to evacuate most of the blocks. It was not at all clear in what direction the evacuees would go, since the Allied noose was getting tighter each day. For most inmates the evacuation ended in a death march. Whoever was unable to keep in step got a bullet in the head. The first block chosen for evacuation was block 22, and it appears that very few survived the bloody march. August miraculously survived because he was hidden by his comrades in the experimental farm where he worked. I never saw him again after the war, and I don't know what happened to my poems and to Kurt's little chef d'oeuvre.

Reaching Out

In April 1944, I could tell that spring had arrived. I could tell it from the snow thawing under my feet and the milder breezes blowing over the Appelplatz. Otherwise, there was not much change. The two trees near the camp gate, leafless and black, continued to look more like gallows than trees, and the birds, proverbial harbingers of spring, showed no inclination to alight in our place. As before, people continued to disappear and to die. Perhaps hunger was claiming more victims than before, because more *mussulmans* (prisoners who had lost the will to live) were rummaging through the discarded garbage pails, while the number of emaciated evacuees brought in from camps in the east was steadily rising. But their arrival kept the rumor mill going. It was said that the Soviet forces had crossed some major rivers in the east, that the Italian army had capitulated, and that the Americans were on their way to Rome. It was even whispered that with God's help there might soon be a second front. A whiff of spring was clearly in the air.

With the passing of time I continued to enlarge my circle of friends. Thanks to Witek I met Jan Zygmunt, a Polish literary scholar and critic who was about twice my age. After the war he enjoyed a considerable career in his homeland, mostly for the services he was glad to perform for the regime. It was said that he was as slippery and slick as an eel. In the camp, however, he was the epitome of courtesy and kindness, and he sounded like a liberal of the old bourgeois school. A lover of French literature, he admired above all the literature of the Poles. He had a special weakness for two novels by authors with almost identical names, Proust's *A la Recherche du Temps Perdu* (*Remembrance of Things Past*) and Prus's *Lalka* (The doll). He could speak for hours about the intricacy of both of their narrative styles, and he claimed that the so-called realistic novel, with its multiple characters, conflicts, and voices, was the nineteenth century's greatest contribution to verbal art.

Jan Zygmunt introduced me in turn to a young Polish poet, Edmund Polak. He was but a few years older than I and worked outside the main camp as a roofer, repairing or covering with shingles the roofs of the huge barracks of the SS. His hands wore the permanent stains of tar, and he liked to show them off as a mark of his trade. In his free time he walked around with a tiny pencil and small pieces of paper on which he scribbled barely legible words. These were his *trouvailles* of rhymes, metaphors, or the beginnings of poems. On Sundays we would meet on the Appelplatz and Polak would read to me some of his latest products. His poems were moving and well made but were all in a minor key; they delivered neither a frisson nor a punch. Around the same time I discovered in the library a slim volume of Rilke's verse. I was overwhelmed by its beauty. "My God!" I thought, "What an artist! And how could I have missed this poetry before?" I savored, like wine, the sound and flow of the words, and I tried to memorize some of the lines while I was trudging along with my heavy loads. My enjoyment of Rilke was heightened by the fact that I was able to share the poems with Polak, who had an excellent knowledge of German. One of them, a little gem of five lines, was our favorite, perhaps because it applied so well to our life:

Der Tod ist gross. Wir sind die seinen
lächelnden Munds.
Wenn wir uns mitten im Leben meinen,
Wagt er zu weinen
Mitten in uns.

Death is great. We are his
With a smile on our face.
When we believe ourselves to be in the midst of life,
He dares to cry
Deep in us.

Polak was working on the libretto for a musical to be performed in one of the Polish blocks. Through him I got to know some of the prospective actors and received a commission to paint the sets. The conductor was to be Tadzio, a Polish pianist and accordionist who had recently been appointed head of the camp orchestra. The main function of the orchestra was to play military marches at the camp's gate during the departure of the working columns and during their return. The members of the orchestra were the best-dressed men in the camp. Some crazy SS man had conceived the idea that they should be dressed in the uniform of the Yugoslav royal guard: they wore red pants and navy blue jackets embroidered with golden braids and golden epaulets. When they marched out to the gate, they looked like a bunch of painted mannequins moving in step. I cultivated my friendship with Tadzio, who recruited some of his musicians when I got around to composing a play. But he did something else as well: he introduced me to the man who would get me a new job.

The man's name was Ignatz. He too was a *Wasserpole* who had been brought to the camp in 1939, that is, right after the German invasion of Poland. Back home he had been a barber, but in the camp he was a medic. He worked in the Little Hospital, or *Revier* 2, an extension of the main hospital, or *Revier* 1. The Little Hospital was located in a long block divided into two parts, each with about fifty beds: one part was for patients with scarlet fever and smallpox, and the other for people with pneumonia, tuberculosis, and bad colds. Because of the infectious nature of the diseases, one could get into the block only by special permission. The Little Hospital employed about ten people: a *kapo*, a *Blockältester*, a *Schreiber*, three medics, and several *Calefactors*. Ignatz was the chief medic, and he performed not only the functions of a nurse but also those of a doctor, since no regular doctor had been assigned to that block. Several times a week a doctor from *Revier* 1 came by to take a look at the patients, but given the nature of the diseases and the lack of effective cures, there was no need for him to stay.

Ignatz had little education but lots of ambition. It was not clear whether he had ever finished high school, but he was determined to become a doctor once the war ended. In the service of this goal he liked to mix with educated people, hoping that some of their knowledge would rub off. They, in turn, respected him for his fearless work with the sick and for his lavish generosity toward friends. Like a Good Samaritan, he would slip a slice of bread or a piece of margarine to a man in need or to one not ashamed to ask. It was the high rate of mortality on the block that made his largesse possible, since he could always put his hands on some leftover bread. Most of it he shared with friends, and some he exchanged for other goods. He took particular care of the cubicle in which he lived and which he treated both as a bedroom and a salon. His bed was covered with a colorful quilt, and in the middle of the room stood a round table and several wooden chairs. Glossy posters covered the walls, featuring the latest airplane models, views of Paris and the Alps, and a picture of the pope or of some Polish saint. From a small photograph nearby peered the round face of Ignatz's sister. In the corner of the room stood a neatly polished potbellied stove. The room was strategically located, as it was separated from the patients by the *Schreibstube* (office) and two cubicles for the staff. Thus Ignatz did not have to worry about the noise made by some of his guests or the groans coming from the hospital area.

To this room were invited some of Ignatz's chosen friends. We usually got together on Sunday afternoons to discuss the news, talk about books, and recite poems. Stimulated by Rilke and encouraged by Polak, I too began to write poetry, this time in Polish, the language I knew best, after all, and the fountainhead of my literary upbringing. Occasionally, Tadzio would come along with three or four violinists to perform classical music.

One fine day Ignatz invited several of us to a party. He wanted to celebrate a special event, he said, namely, his promotion to the position of *Blockältester*. His predecessor, it turned out, had been recruited by the SS to fight for the fatherland. In reality the promotion did not count for much because the *Blockältester* of a hospital performed exactly the same functions as the other medics. But Ignatz took it as a good omen, a further step toward his future career. On Sunday afternoon we arrived in his place, where his genius as an "organizer" was quite apparent. On a white tablecloth were several plates with slices of bread and slivers of margarine on the side. On the stove, a large frying pan sizzled with slices of potato. And, wonder of wonders, amid the potatoes swam chunks of meat, a delicacy that none of us had seen for years—or at least since our arrival in the camp. The meat fried slowly in the pan, emanating a delicious odor and acquiring a golden brown hue. To top it off, Ignatz gave each of us a glass into which he poured a few drops of vodka. We raised our glasses to the host, wishing him the best of health and the not-too-distant attainment of his goals. After the meal, which we consumed all too quickly, Ignatz produced several cigarette butts that he must have secured at considerable cost. The room filled with a cloud of smoke and a most festive air. In that mood we intoned, as is the Polish custom, a few Polish folk songs, such as "Góralu, czy Ci nie żal?" (Mountaineer, are you not sorry?) and "Czerwone jabłuszko" (A red apple).

But in the midst of the merrymaking there came a knock on the door, and in stepped big Bruno, the *Lagerältester*, the *capo dei capi* who hardly ever visited the blocks but whom everyone regarded with awe. He was indeed a big man who associated freely with the SS and who walked around, like them, in a neatly pressed uniform and in officers' boots. He was never seen alone but went around in the company of two corpulent *kapos* and a German shepherd named Max. Now he was alone. After a perfunctory greeting, he turned to Ignatz:

"Ignatz," he asked, "have you seen my dog?"

"Your dog? Which dog?" retorted Ignatz.

"What do you mean 'which dog'?" said Bruno. "My dog Max."

"No, I haven't seen Max," answered Ignatz.

"You see," said Bruno, "the people in the next block said that a night or two ago they heard a faint howling in your block."

"Well, I didn't hear any howling," said Ignatz, "but if you wish, you can look around, both here and outside the *Revier.*"

At this Bruno went over to the section with the patients and came back after a while with a sour face. Then he stepped outside, and we heard him walk around the block several times.

"Max!" he shouted. "Max! Wo bist du denn, Mensch? Max, komm' doch 'raus!" (Where are you, you silly fellow? Max, come out!).

But there was no trace of Max. Bruno returned to our room to bid us good-bye. He was already on the other side of the door when he suddenly came back.

"Ignatz," he said, "it seems to me that there is a smell of meat in the air."

"Meat?" wondered Ignatz. "I cannot smell any meat. Edek, do you smell any meat?" he said, turning to me.

"No," I replied, "I don't smell any meat."

"And you, Tadzio, do you smell meat?"

"No," answered Tadzio, shaking his head.

Bruno stood there perplexed, with a half-open mouth, then left the block without saying good night. We felt sorry for Bruno, but none of us lied. We did not smell the meat because it was in our stomachs, and it was good. The meat was, of course, the dog.

Negotiating a New Job

On several occasions I visited Ignatz by myself. He never failed to treat me to a cup of "coffee" or to ask me about my past. It pained me that I could not unburden myself by telling him the truth. But that truth had not been shared with anyone except Wilhelm and block 22, and I was determined to keep it that way. I had not the slightest doubt that Ignatz was a decent man who would not betray me, even at the risk of his own life. But I told him the same story I told anyone who asked: that I came from a small town in Galicia, where I finished high school; my father had passed away before the war; my mother was a good Catholic but did not go regularly to church; I had worked for about a year for a German outfit in the eastern Ukraine, where I was arrested with a group of Poles. I was confident that no one would bother or be able to verify the facts of my story. The camp at Igrenie, I said, was evacuated in a hurry under the threat of approaching Russian tanks, and the Gestapo of Dnieproderzhinsk had apparently not bothered to forward my full dossier, thinking that they were sending me to my death.

Ignatz did not like to speak of his family, but he complained that he had never had a chance to get a real education. He spoke Polish and German but had problems writing these languages. He complained that he was now more than thirty years old and that he might not be able to fulfill his dream. To become a doctor he would have to learn a number of things: chemistry and anatomy, physics and history, and, above all, Latin, the lingua franca and pride of the medical profession. Listening to that talk, I had the feeling that Ignatz was nursing an idea that might soon turn into a practical proposal. Indeed, one evening he came over to my block. "Listen," he said, "I have an idea. I want you to be my teacher. Every Sunday you can come over to my block to tutor me for an hour or two. In exchange for your lessons, I will see to it that you eat better than a *kapo*." I laughed at the idea. "Ignatz," I said, "the things you want to learn will take more than an hour or two a week to learn, and I will be too tired to teach them to you on Sundays, the only day we can get some rest." But he was not easily put off. Next he approached me with a new idea. "Edward," he said, "how would you like to work in my *Revier* as a *calefactor?*" "Oh, no," I said, "that is not a job for me. I am scared of the sicknesses in your block and would rather remain a porter. At least I get lots of fresh air."

Despite my cavalier pose, I found myself mulling over the proposal, weighing the pros and cons. By leaving the Strumpfstopferei, I would rid myself of heavy loads and the Russians and I would not be exposed to the rains, wind, and nasty Buchenwald fog; nor would I have to stand for hours on the Appel—and perhaps I would get more to eat. But equally strong were the cons: I would be cooped up in a place with hardly anyone to talk to; should I fail as a teacher, I would be out of a job; I would live in a barrack ridden with disease; and in no time, I could contract scarlet fever or TB and die. Moreover, by leaving the Strumpfstopferei I would also lose Wilhelm, my protector and friend. Yet it did not take too long for me to decide. The *Revier* won. It offered the one thing that mattered most at the time: the chance of getting more food.

But what kind of work could I do? I couldn't be a medic and I wouldn't be a *calefactor*. It occurred to me that I could be a *Schreiber*.

The functions of a hospital scribe were to register the incoming sick and to keep their files neatly in order. In fact, the neatness of the files mattered far more than the fate of the sick. Since the camp had no typewriters, the records had to be written in perfect calligraphy, a job for which I had garnered some experience in the ghetto. I could also help with the different languages. Most inmates were foreigners who hardly knew any German, and to expedite their admission it was helpful to speak to them in their native tongue. In addition to German I could speak Polish, Russian, and some French. I told Ignatz that I would be willing to move to his block if he could get me a job as *Schreiber.* The trouble with my offer was that the Little Hospital already had a *Schreiber*, a Czech from Prague whom they liked and who satisfied all their needs. Ignatz treated my proposal as a challenge; he was ready to persuade the block's *kapo* that the *Revier* was badly in need of a second scribe.

The truth is that the *kapo* did not need much persuading. The camp was almost daily getting new arrivals, many of whom were critically ill. Buchenwald contributed its share and, though many kept dying, the demand for beds was always acute. Both *Reviers* were overflowing and there was talk of building an extension, a *Revier* 3. In the meantime, many sick were put on mattresses outside the block, which did not do them any good. Under these circumstances, the Czech could hardly keep up with registering the sick, much less with the desired neatness of the records. In the beginning of May, Ignatz introduced me to the *kapo* of the Little Hospital, who offered me a temporary job—temporary, that is, until I showed that I was worthy of the position of full-time scribe.

Revier Number Two

M y transfer to the new place was swift. Although I knew that I could not expect to get a room to myself, I was somewhat disappointed to be assigned to a cubicle occupied by three other members of the staff and to an upper bunk. However, it beat sleeping in a hall with more than a hundred men. Across from the cubicle was the *Schreibstube*, an austere but fairly cozy office. It was the domain of the *Schreiber*, Zdenek Adla, and was spacious enough to accommodate two desks, a few chairs, and a cot. On the wall was a picture of the Prague castle, and on Zdenek's desk was a photograph of a young woman—his wife.

Zdenek was a well-known illustrator and graphic artist. Like Ignatz, he had been in the camp for more than four years and had learned to stay alive by keeping mostly to himself. He had a pleasant complexion, but he was small, bulky, and balding. His blue eyes looked at the world as if they could not believe what they were seeing, and his gaze turned inward whenever he started to talk. But he did not talk much. He spent most of his time at his desk, leaving the reception of new patients to the medics. It was an exciting experience to watch him at work. With a quick swoop of the pen he would produce letters and figures, breezy and vigorous in their arrangement and shape. When he was done filling out the forms, he arranged the files in alphabetical order, to be ready for inspection by the *kapo* before the roll call. If there was time left, he would pull out a pad on which he drew sketches for posters, portraits of inmates, and imaginary animals. The latter were witty and amusing, if also menacing and mean. Before the Christian holidays he also drew pictures of little girls with round eyes and cherubic smiles, probably as gifts for his Czech friends. Once in a while I bumped into some of them, and it was in their company that I could swear I saw Zdenek smile. It was obvious that he liked to speak mostly to Czechs, and preferably only in Czech. In general, I formed the impression that the Czechs were a clannish bunch who liked to talk only to each other. Zdenek made an exception for one person, Otto, the *kapo* of the block.

On the surface, Otto and Zdenek were completely different types. Otto was thin and tall, while Zdenek was chunky and small; Otto was practical and dry, while Zdenek was an artist and a dreamer. Yet, like Don Quixote and Sancho Panza, they made a perfect pair. Here the comparison ends, for unlike the Spanish couple, they were both taciturn and morose. They could spend hours together without uttering a word, and one felt that they could—and did—at times communicate with each other nonverbally. They had worked for two or three years in the Little Hospital and made it function like a quiet and well-oiled machine. Otto had a room at the far end of the block, but he would come over to the *Schreibstube* several times a day to discuss with Zdenek the operation of the block or to relax on the narrow cot. On and off he would look through the patients' files and at Zdenek's drawings, smiling or nodding his head. However, on most mornings, even before the roll call, he would drop by to report to Zdenek what was going on in the camp and the latest rumors about the course of the war. During these brief tête-à-têtes, I did not exist. The two of them had neither need nor room for a third party.

The summer of 1944 was a period of momentous events, both outside and inside the camp. In May, the Russians had opened a major offensive on the entire length of the eastern front. On June 5, the Allies had taken Rome, and a day later they landed in Normandy. The Poles rose against the Nazis in Warsaw, and from the new transports we learned about the exploits of the maquis in France and the partisans in Yugoslavia. The camp was abuzz with rumors that the German armies were crumbling on all fronts and that we would soon be liberated by either the Americans or the Russians. At this point it did not much matter which group would get to Buchenwald first.

However, the good news was followed by new hardships for the camp. The transports arriving from all parts of Europe could not be accommodated in the old blocks, forcing the SS to open an annex to the main camp. This so-called Little Camp soon filled up with thousands of haggard, worn out, and bewildered new inmates, the majority of whom were Hungarian Jews. Almost overnight the ethnic character of Buchenwald, which had since 1940 been nearly *judenrein* (free of Jews), changed. To avoid mixing the inhabitants of the old camp with the new crowd of Jews, and also to prevent the spread of disease, the SS erected a barbed-wire fence around the entire length of the new site. The newly erected tents could hardly accommodate the vast mass of people, and as they had neither electricity nor running water, many of their inhabitants wound up sleeping in the open, using holes in the ground for toilets, and washing at collective faucets, around which there formed muddy, foul, and impassable lakes. The Little Camp began to look more like a zoo than a ghetto.

With the Hungarians, the camp received its first contingent of children, Jewish boys ranging from ages three to twelve. We were amazed that they were not all killed along with their parents. Three of them wound up in our block with scarlet fever.

As I mentioned, there was not much we could do to fight this disease. The medics applied cold packs to various parts of the body, covered the rosy facial rashes with patches, prepared thin soups with milk substitutes, and waited for the fever to go away. The two older boys, aged nine or ten, recovered after three or four weeks and went back to block 8, which was assigned to the children. The youngest boy, who was five or six, refused to get better. His name was Joseph, and he spoke a blend of Slovak and Polish, a mix he must have acquired in one of the camps. The three of us, Zdenek, Ignatz, and I, had no problem understanding his strange patois, and we soon developed an attachment to the little red-faced orphan. We would apply his packs, feed him soup, and sit by his bed telling him little stories. Even Otto came by several times a day to check on how he was doing. When he began to feel better after a few weeks, we jumped for joy and congratulated ourselves on our success.

Just at that point we got a visit from one of the Nazi doctors, *Hauptsturmführer* Schuler, the head of Pathologie, known for experiments on inmates from which they never survived. Otto and Zdenek, who had known about his business for some time, accompanied him on the block. Schuler approached the boy's bed, took a look at his face, and told Otto that he wanted little Joseph at his outfit as soon as he was better. Otto tried to tell him that the boy had gone through two near-fatal diseases, typhus at Auschwitz and scarlet fever in Buchenwald, and that he would not be much good for any of the treatments Herr Doctor had in mind. But for Schuler the visit was over, and he reminded Otto as he left that he expected to see the boy in a few days. The situation was critical, and we didn't know what to do. Just then I remembered that I had recently met a young Polish chemist who had been working for some time at Pathologie. He was also the one who told me that the inmates employed in that outfit, mostly doctors and chemists, were helping the German doctors in more than one way. In addition to assisting with the experiments, they provided them with cakes of soap for their wives, flagons of perfumes, and bottles of vodka made from the alcohol intended for the hospital and Pathologie. *Hauptsturmführer* Schuler himself owed his doctor's degree to a dissertation on typhus written by one of the inmates. When I got to Pathologie I told my friend about our problem, suggesting that they save little Joseph by offering the *Hauptsturmführer* a few bottles of their exquisite local brew.

"It won't do," said my friend, "*Hauptsturmführer* Schuler is unaware that we have a distillery, and if he finds out it may cost us not only the distillery but our heads. On top of it, he is a fanatical Nazi who cannot be bribed. But do not worry," he added," your *kapo* Otto has already been here and together with my *kapo*, Gustav, they might come up with something to save the boy. As a matter of fact, your *kapo* left only a while ago and he seemed to be in a cheerful temper."

It took us only a few days to learn what Otto and Gustav had come up with. It was an injection of phenol or milk. After a few days at Pathologie, little Joseph developed a frightfully high fever, and the idea of submitting him to any sort of experiment had to be dropped. He was subsequently transferred to *Revier 1*, where he stayed for another three or four weeks. I saw him again when he, with several other children, showed up at my musical. I was delighted, for I could tell by his vigorous clapping that he had recovered and was enjoying my play.

We had barely gotten over the trauma of little Joseph's brush with death when *Revier* 2 was hit by another disaster, this time from the outside.

One morning Ignatz dropped in to visit me while Zdenek was opening a letter from Prague. One could tell from the changes in his face that the news was not good. He went over the letter three or four times, threw down his pen, shoved aside the pile of forms, and ran out of the block without saying a word. He returned in the evening in the company of Otto and withdrew right away to his room. Otto came by after the roll call to tell Ignatz and me what had happened. Zdenek's wife had written him that she had annulled their marriage, as she was about to marry another man. After four years, she wrote, she got tired of waiting. The next day Zdenek showed up in the office distraught and disheveled, as if he had not slept a whole night. I rushed up to tell him how sorry I was for his loss. He muttered some words with a look of annoyance, as if I were partly to blame for the desertion of his wife.

In the meantime our block was bursting at the seams. The growing number of sick made it impossible to separate them by disease, especially since even the doctors lacked the proper medical terms for some of the illnesses. Being responsible for the registration of the patients, I simplified my task by classifying them into three groups: scarlet fever, smallpox, and "internal." In the last group I included bleeding ulcers, lacerated legs, swollen necks, and stomach and chest wounds. The patients couldn't care less; they knew that the *Revier* was not a place to which they were sent to be cured. Because of the shortage of beds, we put some of them on cots and some on mattresses between the beds.

Faced with the danger of overcrowding and general confusion, Otto tried to get rid of the dead as soon as it was possible to tell that they were really dead. He arranged for the boys of the crematorium, the so-called *Totenkommando*, to show up at the *Revier* at the crack of dawn. By then our own *Calefactors* would have collected all the corpses they could find and would have stacked them outside in a pile; they then helped the *Totenkommando* load them into the two-wheeled carts. They transported them in haste, with dead from other blocks picked up along the way, to their final fate: the gray and black clouds rising from the bulky chimney of Buchenwald's crematorium.

However, the *kapo's* plans to make room for the new arrivals did not always work out. This became apparent in the case of the fifteen Danish policemen who were delivered, totally naked, to our block sometime in the middle of July. As there was no room in the block, we placed them outside on the grass or on low-folding cots. Unconscious and mute, they lay there with just enough life to try to shoo away the swarms of flies, to scratch their festering skins, and to play with their genitals. The rows of tall, blond, handsome, and still fairly muscular men gasping for the last breath of life under a broiling sun was something to behold, and a number of passing inmates, including some *mussulmans*, stopped to gawk. The sight of the *mussulmans*, who could barely stand on their feet, watching the flower of Denmark's manhood in their last spasms of life, made palpable the pathos and paradox of what it was to live and to die in the camp. With a bit of luck, the former, with their spindly legs, protruding hip and shoulder bones, eyes buried deep in their sockets, and necks like those of plucked roosters, could go on dragging their hollowed bodies around for another few weeks, while the Danish policemen were all dead in a few days.

The Lessons

Through all these events I did not forget for a minute why I found myself in the Little Hospital and that Ignatz was waiting for me to get started on our scholarly work. However, the needs of our patients forced us to put off our studies for a number of weeks.

Ignatz was probably the most overworked medic in the camp. He would personally treat open wounds, sit by the beds of patients at night, clean their infested skins, and listen to the last beat of their hearts. All this he did with stoic calm, as if he had a pact with Death to leave him alone. He lost his composure only when someone whom he had tended for some time suddenly died. Good Catholic that he was (to judge by the picture of the pope or of a Polish saint hanging in his room), he would get into an argument with heaven verging on blasphemy.

"Almighty God!" he would mutter, "Couldn't you have spared such a good and innocent life?" Or "Holy Virgin, Mother of Mercy! Couldn't you have interceded on behalf of such a sweet and good-looking young man?"

As Ignatz had predicted, we could study no more than one or two hours a week, mostly on Sundays. But even on Sunday it was not easy to get down to work, for there were always the sick to attend to and the dead to be removed from the block. This was also the only day that we could meet friends and go out for a walk on the Appelplatz. But what caused me some real strain was that I did not quite know what kind of knowledge I was to share with my student. Ignatz had not even finished public school, yet he had gotten it into his head that he was going to be a doctor. He spoke Polish with a strong Silesian accent, sprinkled with German phrases and words. We agreed it would be best to begin my instruction with history and Latin. Latin mattered to Ignatz a great deal, for he saw it as a gateway to his future career. There was not much else I could really teach him.

I decided to begin our Latin lessons with the study of a few memorable phrases. Educated men, especially educated Poles, I told Ignatz, like to show off their education by tossing around Latin sayings; now he too would be able to shine in the company of our sophisticated friends by reciting some Latin. I figured that by teaching the sayings, I could also impart to him the rudiments of Latin grammar, as well as some facts concerning their historical and cultural background.

The first saying I wrote down on a piece of paper was *suum cuique,* for that was the Latin source of the inscription that greeted us all upon the arrival in Buchenwald: *Jedem das Seine.* The meaning it conveyed was that we deserved what we got. Next I wrote *Primum edere, deinde philosophari* (First we eat, and then we philosophize). Ignatz showed an instant grasp of the relevance of this saying to our situation, and he nodded his head in recognition when I topped it with another saying, coined by a German philosopher: *Der Mensch ist was er isst* (Man is what he eats). This saying captured the human condition in the camp better than any other, because the quality—indeed, the very essence—of a man could be estimated by the quantity of food he managed to put daily into his stomach. These sayings I topped off with several others that had a bearing on our existence. Foremost among them was *Memento mori* (Remember death) and *Homo homini lupus* (Man to man is a wolf). I told my disciple that the latter saying had been attributed to an English philosopher who taught that in his primitive state man did not differ much from an animal, and that he gave up his wolfish behavior only when he learned to live with other men under a strong ruler and in an organized state. Now Ignatz could judge for himself whether our present conditions under a strong ruler and in an organized state confirmed the philosopher's optimism. Philosophers, I told him, were good at coining memorable Latin phrases, and that was why intelligent people admired them and liked to quote them. For example, in France there was Descartes, a mathematician and philosopher who believed that we exist because we think. His saying was *Cogito, ergo sum.* What we think about does not much matter, as long as we think. Another philosopher, this time the Englishman Locke, maintained, on the other hand, that the brain remains a *tabula rasa* (clean slate) until it received an infusion of outside impressions. Latin sayings, I pointed out, also provide historical wisdom and are quite useful when one finds oneself in a bind. For example, when one is faced with some life-and-death decision, one can repeat, after the great Roman warrior Julius Ceasar, *Alea iacta est* (The die is cast), and, as it did for him, it may help one cross his Rubicon. Another Roman statesman made up the sentence *Ceterum censeo Cartaginem delendam esse* (And yet I think that Carthage must be destroyed), a quite useful saying if a person wants something nasty to happen to his enemies. Another nifty expression was *cave canem* (beware of the dog), a warning the Romans wrote in front of their houses.

All this wisdom I tried to impart to my disciple. I had a much harder time with the grammar, because Ignatz could not learn the meaning nor memorize the names of the Latin tenses, cases, or moods. He was puzzled by the number of declensions and conjugations and considered them a waste of time and energy, an opinion I could not but share. After a while we decided to give up on the grammar, and I told Ignatz that I would feel rewarded as his teacher if he could simply memorize a few of the Latin sayings. But on this score we didn't do too well either. Of all the sayings, Ignatz remembered best *cave canem* and *homo homini lupus.* When he recited them for the first time in the company of my friends, they were surprised and amused, for they never suspected him of knowing any Latin. However, when he repeated them each time they showed up in our block, they thought that these phrases were intended for them, and they were no longer amused. Ignatz himself developed a strange attitude toward our friends. He accused them of snobbery and elitism, claiming that they purposely discussed things he did not understand, and he felt that I ignored him whenever they came by. He became altogether too possessive and jealous for my taste. At first I tried to ignore his barbs, but then I began to resent his accusing tone and complaints. We agreed to drop our work on Latin for a while and to turn our efforts toward the study of history.

It so happened that at that time, around the middle of 1944, I stumbled upon two English books in the library, Bernard Shaw's *Saint Joan* and Dickens's *A Tale of Two Cities.* The unexpected finds stimulated me to resume my study of English, a subject I had neglected since the murderous *akcja* in the Lwów ghetto. The two books stayed with me until the liberation of the camp and became my principal guides into the subtleties of the English language. I read them over and over, trying to memorize words, phrases, and entire pages. Dickens equipped me with my highfalutin vocabulary and antiquated idioms. When, after the liberation, I became an interpreter for an American outfit in Erfurt (near Buchenwald), I tickled the GIs with such phrases as, "What o'clock do you make it?" "I grieve to inform you," "Blessed if I know!" "I can't quite apprehend you," and "Pray take a seat." Luckily for me, I had also met in the camp a young Frenchman by the name of Pierre, who had spent several years in Canada and who helped me with the pronunciation and translation of some English words. I still think of you, Pierre, with affection, for your help with English and for teaching me a few French songs popular at that time!

As the two books dealt with two major events in the history of Europe, I used them as a springboard for the teaching of history. Ignatz had heard of the French Revolution, but not of Saint Joan. I told him that she was a peasant girl who heard strange voices, led the French troops in battles against the English, had King Charles crowned at the cathedral of Rheims, was burned at the stake by the Church as a heretic, and was later beatified and made into a saint by the same Church. I enjoyed Shaw's play mostly for the description of the hypocrisy of the churchmen, the crudity of the English, and the perfidy of Joan's compatriots. Otherwise I found the play too garrulous, too cerebral, and too cute. Joan herself is as flat as a piece of cardboard, and Shaw cannot make up his mind whether she was a Protestant like Hus, a naïve monarchist, an ardent patriot, or an obsessed female.

Dickens made a far stronger impression on me with his *Tale of Two Cities*, a historical narrative that manages to deliver a strong emotional punch. The probity of Sydney Carton and his trip with the little girl to the guillotine are unforgettable for their simplicity and for the pathos of human sacrifice. For days I kept mumbling the words recited by Carton during this ride: "He that believeth in me, though he were dead, yet shall he live; and whosoever liveth and believeth in me, shall never die." But as much as I liked the story, I disliked Dickens's treatment of the Revolution, with its touch of Francophobia and air of British superiority. The whole world-shaking revolutionary event is looked at through the frame of the guillotine in the midst of a vindictive, bloodthirsty, and hollering mob, led by a knife-wielding tigress named Therese Defarge. Not a word is written about the philosophers who had prepared the Revolution, the growing importance of the third class, the collapse of the feudal estates, and the internecine feuds of the revolutionary leaders themselves. The real tragedy of France, I lectured my tutee, was the taste for war and conquest that accompanied the rise of the modern French state and the creation of a military establishment set on devouring all the countries of Europe. The Napoleonic wars cost *la douce France* almost as many dead as the combined casualties of its opponents. What is worse, I said, is that under the banner of *liberté* and *egalité* France had infected all other nations of Europe, and most of all Germany, with the pestilence of nationalism, leading to wars and orgies of slaughter that have never come to an end, the price of which we are still paying in this camp. Lucky, I said, are the countries that were splintered and small, such as classical Greece or Italy during the Renaissance, which, unable to build empires, built academies and churches, leaving the glory of conquest to such giants as Rome or the Ottoman Turks.

My student was not very happy with my conclusions. The history of Poland, he argued, makes null and void my entire theory. For there was a country mighty and large that, at the height of its power, accorded equal rights to its citizens and brought Western culture to the steppes of the Ukraine and to the pagan Lithuanians. It was clear to me that Ignatz, the good Catholic and patriotic Pole that he was, had never heard about the seventeenth-century uprising of the Ukrainian Cossaks against the Poles or the bitterness of the Lithuanians over the virtual Polonization of their country. And, of course, I was not going to enlighten him about the treatment the Jews had received over the ages from the Poles, and especially from the Polish Catholic Church. Instead, I shifted our history lessons to the Greeks, to the golden age of Pericles: their magnificent art, their schools of philosophy, and the Greek fascination with all forms of love. Thus we went on for a few more weeks, until new events brought our lessons dramatically to an end.

The Air Raid

One such major event was the bombing of Buchenwald on August 24, 1944. For several months we were able to watch the ribbon-like contrails of Allied squadrons flying high over the camp to their various destinations. We looked up at them, hoping that they would release the fury of their bombs on the German cities and industrial centers while making sure that none of them fell on our camp. For what would have been the use of such a raid? Buchenwald was in the very heart of Germany, and even if the electrified barbed wires were destroyed, we could not hope to hide in any of the nearby forests or to find shelter in any of the surrounding villages or towns. We would have been picked out by the SS like pigeons, if not killed beforehand with pitchforks by the civilians. Our only salvation was liberation by the Allies.

One beautiful afternoon we noticed the silver glitter of an approaching fleet that suddenly turned around and swooped down over the camp in several runs. Then it came down very low, dropping incendiary bombs as it flew over the munitions factories, the quarry, the SS barracks, the garages, and the stables that were all located on the other side of the camp. In no time all these installations, including the Gustloff Werke and G.I. Farben factories that employed hundreds of inmates, burst into flames, with black clouds billowing up to the sky and tongues of fire licking the chimneys, roofs, and walls of the factories. Nervous SS men were running from their barracks, some of them with their dogs and others with children in their arms. Columns of inmates were marched out by guards in black uniforms (the garb of Ukrainian and Vlasovite troops) to help extinguish the fires, while groups of *mussulmans* gathered near the Kommandantur (near the camp's gate) to gape in wonder at the unusual spectacle. When it was all over, we learned that the only building in the camp to be brushed by the fire was a wall of the crematorium that was close to the barbed wire fence. But there were many dead and wounded among the SS, as well as among the prisoners working in the Gustloff Werke. Some bodies were never recovered; they were either buried in the rubble or burned beyond recognition. After the air raid we also discovered that behind the SS barracks was a special enclosure called *Fichtenhain* (pine orchard) that housed a number of European notables, such as Leon Blum; Ernst Thalmann; Princess Mafalda, daughter of Vittorio Emmanuele III, the Italian king; and Rudolf Breitscheid, head of the German Social Democrats. The last three perished as a result of the raid, although there were rumors in the camp that the Nazis used the opportunity to execute Thalmann soon after the attack.

For several days there was a great deal of activity outside the camp's gates. Truckfuls of SS and black-uniformed guards were coming and going, columns of inmates were marched out to remove the rubble, and workers were brought in from Weimar to fix the roofs of the SS barracks and ammunition factories. Because of the disappearance of some inmates and the arrival of new transports, the roll calls lasted about twice as long as usual. But soon everything returned to normal.

I couldn't feel sorry for the SS nor for Mafalda, but for days I couldn't get out of my mind one inmate who perished in that raid, my friend Marian, the Jewish-Polish peasant from Lwów who had given me some slices of bread and bought my two coins shortly after my arrival in the camp. Our encounters had been brief and infrequent because there was not very much we could talk about and because Marian didn't like to be seen in my company by his very Polish and very Catholic friends. We would walk around in a remote part of the Appelplatz while he told me stories of his life before his arrest. Thus I learned that this goyish-looking man had been sent in his youth to a yeshiva, because his father had wanted him to be a rabbi. Although he had been a good student, by the age of sixteen or seventeen he had developed an unhealthy liking for the shikses in town and would sneak out at night from the shul to gratify his yearnings. Denounced by another student, he was kicked out of the yeshiva and returned to Lwów, where he went into business with an older man as a chicken and egg farmer. In the fall of 1939, when the Soviets nationalized the farm, Marian decided to remain as one of the members of the collective. Another member was a Ukrainian girl with whom he fell in love and married. During the withdrawal of the Soviet army, they managed to get away to her birthplace, a village near Kamenetz Podolsk. The wife and Marian's "good" face helped him to get his Aryan papers, his very Christian first name, and the respect of his neighbors. Together with his wife he would attend services in the local church, although he would also say the Jewish morning prayers and fast on the Day of Atonement. He was arrested by mere chance at the market of Kamenetz Podolsk while he was trying to change money. He also got involved in money changing in the camp, albeit on a greatly reduced scale. He had confessed to me that the two gold pieces I gave him were still in his possession, for in one way or another, he explained, he always managed to finagle a few pieces of bread. In fact, during my work in the *Revier* 2 I myself was able to slip him some pieces of bread that were left over because of the high mortality rate in our block. Marian was an

amusing fellow and a great talker, who liked to lard his stories with Yiddish expressions and idioms. I was very fond of him; it irked me that a
man of his ingenuity and wit, and one with such a perfect Aryan face,
was wiped out for no reason in the American-led raid. This, I thought,
was ironic, brutal, and unjust. But in Buchenwald we could not mourn for
long: people came and people went. At the same time, I could not help
wondering what happened to the money Marian must have tucked away.

Block 61

Another major event in my life was the opening of a new hospital,
an extension of the main *Revier*, in block 61. For more than five
months—that is, from the end of October until the day of our liberation
on April 11, 1945—this was to be my workplace and my new residence.

It was a rainy day when I was summoned by Otto to his room. I knew
that something was in the offing, since I had never before had the honor
of seeing even his room. "Stankevitz," he began, stressing the initial syl-
lable of my name with an exaggerated German accent (rhyming with
Clausewitz), "the people of *Revier 1* have appointed you to a new job. You
will be the *Schreiber* in the soon-to-open *Revier* in block 61. The block will
start functioning the moment the carpenters finish putting up the bunks
and the roofers cover the roof with shingles. In the meantime you may
collect your things and get ready to move."

The notion of "collecting my things" was Otto's idea of a joke, since
my worldly possessions consisted of two library books, a few drawings,
and a sheaf of loose papers. The news of my forthcoming move nonethe-
less came as a shock. I was somewhat aware that my time in the Little
Hospital was up. Otto had never liked me, Zdenek liked only Otto and
his Czech pals, and Ignatz had given up on me as a teacher and had taken
a dislike to my friends. I was sure that the idea of my transfer had come
from Otto himself, though on this, as in all other matters, he must have
consulted Zdenek. Ignatz was probably left in the dark, since his opinion
did not carry any weight. I knew that my transfer could only be to some-

thing worse. What added to my distress was that I was not even aware that they were building a new *Revier.* I left Otto's room glum and despondent. I had gotten used to my cubicle, to the *Schreibstube,* and to the daily routine. I had thought that I was doing a good job: I was quick with the interviews of new patients and kept the files in good order. After the initial shock, I tried to console myself any way I could. Perhaps, I thought, the new block really was in need of a *Schreiber* with my calligraphic and linguistic skills. Maybe I would not have to attend to the sick and to the carrying out of the dead. Maybe I would be my own boss.

After my conversation with Otto, I was anxious to see what was happening with the new block—where it was being built and what kind of a hospital it was going to be. I was told that it was located at the very edge of the camp near the wires separating it from the Little Camp. The first time I ventured out to take a look at the place was in the late evening after the roll call. It was getting dark, and a cold wind was beginning to blow through the alleys separating the blocks, hitting me in the face. To get to my destination I had to pass a number of blocks. To keep up my spirits I hummed the tune to the Verlaine poem, whose opening lines Shimmel had recited for me a few days before his death: "Et je m'en vais au vent mauvais / qui m'emporte / De ci de la, pareil à / la feuille morte."

The wooden structure I reached was still in the works: it lacked doors and windows, and early stars were visible through the roof. However, the bunks were all in place, forming two long rows on both sides of the block, broken up on one side by a room for the *kapo* and on the other side by two cubicles for the *Calefactors.* The *Schreibstube*—my future residence—was almost all done. It had a door leading to the main hall and a little window looking into a vestibule that had room for about ten people. Outside the main entrance was a little square that resembled a loading area. This space was apparently intended for the overflow of patients who would have to wait their turn before being admitted into the reception room. Otherwise block 61 looked like all the other blocks except for a few peculiar features. Behind the window of the *Schreibstube* there was a narrow door leading to an annex adjacent to the building, but to which there was no entrance from inside the block. The only way to get to the annex was through the vestibule, although it took me some time to realize that a real gate stood on the other side of the annex.

A few days later I came again to check on the progress of the barrack. Now it was almost all done, with the windows and doors in place. But what distinguished it even more from the other blocks was a barbed wire fence around the main block and a high wooden fence separating the annex from the Little Camp. Once the structure was finished, it became known that block 61 would house dysentery cases, and in no time was it named the *Totenblock*. The name rubbed off on me, too, and I became known as the *Totenschreiber*.

Wenn wir uns mitten im Leben meinen

My *Schreibstube* was a cozy little place. I worked in it, ate in it, and slept in it. Unlike the patients, who crawled or were shoved into the three levels of bunks with a single blanket to each man, I had a cot with a clean sheet, a pillow, and several blankets. Most bunks were already filled when I moved into my room, and the dossiers of the patients were brought to me by a courier from the main *Revier*. All I had to do was move from bunk to bunk to match the name of its occupant with that on the form. To begin with, we had about a hundred men and were ready to receive at least another hundred. But in a very short time we got about three times that number.

Dysentery is a mean disease, and its reputation among the inmates was not much better than that of typhus. Buchenwald was lucky to have eluded typhus, which had killed thousands in the ghettos and in other camps, but the scourge of dysentery made up for this. While the former was carried by lice, the latter resulted from crowding, dirt, contaminated food, and the miseries of hunger. The only remedy our hospital could offer was charcoal, so that one could tell the victims by the black smudges covering their mouths or entire faces. They reminded me of the clowns I used to see as a boy in the Warsaw circus who had painted their faces black or red depending on whether they were imitating a Negro or

an American Indian. The black smudges made the sick look funny and
pathetic. But in the middle of their faces were eyes glowing like dying
cinders, expressing anger, despair, or total resignation. The distinctive
and unmistakable feature of the block was its smell: it was enough to
cross the door leading from the vestibule to the main hall to be over-
powered by the combined odor of feces and a chlorine disinfectant.
White stains from the chlorine splashed over the floor, and the wooden
bunks contrasted with the darkness of their interiors. Given the narrow-
ness of the bunks, a person could hardly tell one patient from another.
The block was off limits to outsiders, while the insiders had to live day
and night with the obnoxious smell. Block 61 deserved the nickname of
Totenblock more than any other *Revier*, for the patients assigned to it were
not expected to last more than a week: many died in a day or two; few
got out on their own feet. One of my smart-aleck friends suggested that
I put up a sign over the window of the *Schreibstube*: "Lasciate ogni sper-
anza voi ch'entrate" (Abandon all hope you who enter).

The empty bunks did not wait long to be filled. The new patients
came from a number of camps, though the majority came from
Auschwitz. It is likely that most of them became sick during the transport, for otherwise they would have never left Auschwitz; they would
have wound up in its own crematorium. Their arrival created general
confusion in our block. Many could hardly stand on their feet; some fell
before they stepped into the vestibule and had to be dragged from there
to their bunks. What aggravated the situation was that these men, all of
them Hungarian Jews, were utterly undisciplined. They pushed and
shoved, shouted and cried, all in Hungarian, the language they insisted
on speaking even when they had a perfectly good knowledge of German. On top of this, they were incapable of giving you a straight answer.
When I asked for their date of birth, they would tell me their profession,
and when I asked for their place of birth, they would start telling me
about the children and wives they had lost in Hungary or in their wanderings through the camps. These interviews frayed my nerves and gave
me bad dreams. As a result I developed an irrational aversion to the Hungarians and their totally incomprehensible language.

For two or three weeks we operated without a *kapo*, but suddenly he showed up. He was about forty or forty-five, with the bearing of a trucker or a longshoreman. Broad in the shoulders, with tufts of reddish hair around his glistening, bald pate, deep-set eyes, and a menacing look, he summoned us—his staff—to his room, located in the middle of the block. He introduced himself as Rudi, while the seven of us—two medics, four *Calefactors*, and a *Schreiber*—stood at attention. The medics were Czechs, while the *Calefactors* included two Poles, a Serb, and a Russian. The Russian, a boy of about seventeen named Kolja, in time became my helper, friend, and teacher of Russian. The *kapo* addressed us briefly. We were all, he said, in the same boat, and he expected discipline and our complete collaboration. When he finished he said, "Abtreten," the way the *Scharführers* dismissed the inmates after the roll calls. His little speech and the way he dismissed us provoked an antipathy for him that I let grow and ripen with every passing week. It was also apparent from the very first day that Rudi didn't care for anyone on his staff, perhaps because we were all Slavs. But he cared even less for the patients, and he let us all know why. He hated them for being Jews, for being Hungarian, and for being sick—in that order. The chosen time for his philosophical perorations was after lunch. A former laborer, he lacked the sophistication of Alfred, my former *kapo* of block 41, and in talking about the Jews he did not cite Marx. But he was sure that the Jews were responsible for the Treaty of Versailles and the miseries that had since befallen the German nation. Had it not been for Jewish capital and intrigues, he asserted, the Germans would have never fallen so low as to elect Hitler as their Führer, a former house painter who had led them from defeat to defeat. Rudi had also read that the Hungarians had come from Asia, were a half-nomadic tribe, and were therefore treacherous and mean. As for the sick, they were responsible for their own troubles. Had they not eaten the filth thrown out from the kitchens or the potato peels retrieved from the garbage cans, they wouldn't have come down with this disease that soils the floor and poisons the air. To demonstrate the strength of his convictions, Rudi demanded that the patients clean themselves and their bunks with mops and buckets of water. Only the hopelessly ill were to be helped by the staff.

As in the Little *Revier*, we were up at five in the morning, counting the patients in the bunks and extracting the dead. The head count was the duty of the *kapo*, but Rudi had asked me to help him, and after a while he left it entirely to me. Being afraid of making a mistake, I recruited Kolja to move with me along the bunks. Rudi himself delivered the list of patients to the main *Revier* before the beginning of the roll call. Between seven and eight o'clock the staff cleaned the bunks, distributed the food and the charcoal, and carried out the dead. As *Totenschreiber* I was relieved of these duties, while Rudi took pride in supervising the activities of his staff. Every once in a while he would find something wrong with a bunk, shout at a patient, or help him on the way to the toilet with a push or a kick. His favorite insults for the sick were "Arschloch," "Spitzbube," and "Hundsfott."

The lads of the *Totenkommando* showed up with their two-wheeled cart by nine or ten, depending on the amount of business they had at the other *Reviers*. Our dead—piles of protruding bones, elongated necks, and grotesque heads—were lying in the little piazza in front of the block, ready to be picked up. The incoming patients were scheduled to arrive by ten, but if they came earlier or the lads with their two-wheeled cart were late, the new arrivals had an opportunity to see how they themselves would look in a week or two. The lads from the *Totenkommando* were known to me from the Little *Revier*. They were sturdy and efficient fellows with a weird sense of humor. "Your block," they said to me, "is our best provider. It beats the other *Reviers* both in the number of units and the promptness of the delivery."

The two fellows were Poles, and we chatted from time to time, mostly about our related jobs. But one day I got to observe them in action more closely. It was around nine or ten in the evening, when all the lights were out, that they showed up with their cart in front of my block. This time they came not to pick up, but to deliver a patient. Sprawled out on the deck of the cart was a bear of a man, his head dangling from the end of the cart. They lifted him on both sides with their big arms, dragged him into the reception room, and dropped him on the floor. I looked at him, trying to make out his face, but it was swollen and covered with bruises. Blood was splashed over his half-naked body. "Register him," said one of the Poles, "and put in tomorrow's date as the time of his death. And you need not bother to get him a bunk. We'll take him away as soon as we are done. And now close the door and the window of your cubicle and leave us alone." I did what they asked but curiosity got the better of me. I put my eyes to a crack in the wall to see what was going on. The man on the floor was half-conscious but breathed heavily, spitting out blood with each breath. The bigger of the two fellows jumped on his chest, but the breathing went on just like before. The smaller guy kicked him in his stomach and balls, and I heard something like a groan coming from the man's chest. But he was still breathing. Then one of the lads ran out and came back with a short wooden board. They placed it across the man's neck, putting themselves on the opposite sides and swinging back and forth like on a seesaw. Suddenly the breathing stopped and there was the sound of gurgling, like a death rattle. Then I saw the sudden violent jerk, and the man was dead. The next morning, when the cart of the *Totenkommando* rolled by, I asked the fellows about the man of the previous night. "Oh," they said, "he was a *kapo* in another camp; justice had to be done." I realized that I should not ask any further questions, but I thought of Ivan, the *kapo* from Igrenie who was stoned upon our arrival in the camp. Buchenwald was meting out justice the prisoners' way.

Yet the lads of the *Totenkommando* did not know what was going on under their own noses, more specifically in the annex located behind block 61. All they knew was that it had a separate entrance facing the Little Camp, and that it was off limits even to them. On my side, I could tell that the annex had a visitor every other day, if not every single day. He was a tall and round-bellied *Hauptsturmführer* who, dressed in a doctor's smock, entered the annex through the narrow door to the left of my *Schreibstube*. He was apparently the only person who had a key to that door. He would show up around two or three in the afternoon and strut majestically across the vestibule to his door without nodding his head or saying a word. His very gait inspired fear, and we all got out of the way the moment we saw him coming. He would stay in the annex an hour or two and leave through the same door with the same unhurried and measured step with which he had arrived. I knew that he did not come to the annex to take a nap or read a book. But what was he up to? It took me some time to find out. I learned the big secret from my friend in Pathologie: the fat doctor was an executioner. He dispatched inmates with a needle of air shot into their necks. I also learned that the corpses were removed from the annex in the middle of the night, and that among them were important prisoners of war as well as political prisoners who had been in Buchenwald and in other camps for a long time. The whole thing seemed to me paradoxical. The butchers of Auschwitz and Buchenwald, who had openly murdered millions of Jews, developed a curious sensitivity when it came to important military or political figures; their deaths were to be hidden forever from public view.

Throughout the fall, our block functioned without a hitch. People were coming and going, usually not on their own. About 50 percent of the patients were pulled out from the bunks each morning, their desiccated and dangling bodies carried like bundles of firewood to the little square outside the block. From there, they were shipped to stoke the Buchenwald ovens. Most of the dying took place at night, and it was also at night that some of our local dramas occurred. For example, one patient tried to steal a blanket from another, starting a ruckus that woke up the entire block. Another night we woke up to incredible screams: one man was trying to pull out the golden teeth from his neighbor's mouth, and the victim was screaming as if he was being murdered. Rudi was the first one on the scene. He dragged the thief from his bunk, hit him in the face, and left him groaning, half-dead on the floor. It was the attacker who soon died, while the intended victim recovered and left the block on his own.

One early morning sometime in December, my own lack of attention got me into trouble when the morning roll call got all messed up. What happened was that when the *Blockführer* added up the figures of the men assembled on the Appelplatz, they appeared to be one inmate short. This could mean only one of two things: either there was a mistake in the count or, less likely, a prisoner had escaped. The SS men deliberated for a while and then ordered a second count. A light snow was covering the ground, and the thousands of inmates stood at attention, shivering in the cold. When the second count yielded the same result, the order went out to count the sick in the three hospitals. It was at that point that Rudi, accompanied by an *Oberscharführer*, came running to our block. They pulled off the blankets from each bunk and after a while discovered the missing prisoner. It was a man who in some mysterious way had slipped over to the bed of his neighbor. I missed him in my count because he had been covered from head to foot by a blanket, and because he was all skin and bones. After the discovery of my mistake, I felt both guilty and ashamed, and I expected the worst. But nobody came after me, nor after anyone else. The whole incident simply blew over. As fate would have it, however, Rudi himself remained on the block only another week or two. His sudden departure, just like his sudden appearance, remained a mystery to me, which, like so many other mysteries in the camp, nobody bothered to explain. Rudi was never replaced, and we managed to cope without a *kapo*.

Life Goes On

Toward the end of November I began to work on a musical that was to be performed in one of the Polish blocks. Such vaudevillelike shows were given almost every Sunday in one or another of the blocks, where they attracted visitors from all over the camp, including the children and some officers of the SS. The latter probably came more to keep an eye on what was going on in the blocks than to enjoy the plays.

Block 21, my old Polish block, had produced several such plays. For one that was written by my friend Polak, I was commissioned to do the sets. I painted a tropical landscape of several palm trees planted on a sandy seashore against a dark blue sky. The author was one of the main actors. He was dressed up in a long straw skirt and a wig of the same material. Tadzio and his musicians (playing fiddle, bassoon, cello, and drum) opened up with a mazurka that soon turned into a dance performed with reckless gyrations by Polak to the beat of Hawaiian drums. Several men with their faces painted black joined in the dance, which unexpectedly turned again into a mazurka. The whole thing was capped with a few Polish songs delivered by a group of four or five men. The musical was a tremendous success.

Polak asked me to write the next Polish play, and I had in mind something quite different from his. I wanted neither exotic dances nor popular Polish songs. I was thinking of a musical that would reflect life in the camp as interpreted in song by the members of its various nationalities, and with appropriate melodies for each group. Thus, the song sung by the Russian would identify a Russian, the song of the Pole, a Pole, that of the Dane, a Dane, and so on. The tunes were to be excerpts from classical, national, or popular music that most people in the audience were likely to know. In this way, I figured, the show would be attractive not only to the Poles but also to members of the other nationalities who might show up for the play. Although most of the lyrics were to be in Polish, I wanted the true appeal of the play to reside, as in opera, in the power of the music and the skill of the musicians, rather than in the performance of the actors. In fact, there was not to be any action at all, except perhaps in the final song, to be delivered by a group of children. Each of the actors would deliver a solo performance and move along the stage, like a figure popping out from a cuckoo clock. I assumed that since most of the lyrics were to be in Polish, I could permit myself certain liberties, for which I would pay dearly if they were understood by one of the visiting SS.

It took us several Sundays to rehearse the show and to arrange the sets. The main dramatis personae were a *Wasserpole* appearing in the role of Hamlet, armed with a shovel and singing the opening bars of Beethoven's Fifth Symphony; a Russian dressed in a torn fur coat and singing "Volga, Volga" (a song that could remind people of Stalingrad); a Pole singing to the tune of "Warszawianka" (a revolutionary song going back to the czarist times); a Spaniard singing "Carmela" (the Republican hit of the civil war); and two or three others. The only feminine voice (that of a boy) was to come from behind the darkened stage, as if from a faraway place, singing "J'attendrai, / le jour et la nuit / J'attendrai toujours, mon amour...," a French song brought to the camp by the most recent French arrivals, the lyrics of which I had learned from my friend Pierre.

For years I have retained in my memory the lines that opened and concluded my musical.

The first to appear was the tall and handsome Silesian Pole, who was dressed up as Hamlet in a broad Basque beret, with a shovel for a sword and a broad black belt around his waist. He was the only actor whose soliloquy was matched by the response of a chorus hidden behind the stage. He sang:

> Czemuż ja tu? Za jaki grzech?
> O, co za pech męczyć się tu!
> Znosić tu głód,
> Nędzę i smród,
> Nie zbawi mnie tu żaden już cud
> Oj, oj, ginie moj ród . . .

and the chorus responded:

> Nie płacz, miły książę duński,
> Nie załamuj się,
> Za górami, za lasami
> Świta nowy dzień,
> Wkrótce w dowód twego męstwa
> Wrócisz do swojego księstwa,
> Wielkim panem będziesz znów!

> Why am here? For what kind of sin?
> What a misfortune to be in this mess,

To suffer hunger,
Squalor and stench
No miracle is going to save me,
Oh, oh, and my line will die out . . .

Chorus:

Do not cry, sweet Danish prince,
Do not despair;
Behind the mountains, behind the forests
There dawns a new day.
In recognition of your courage
You'll return to your principality
And you'll be again a great lord!

The play ended with a march by several boys, the Polish-Jewish boys who were housed in block 8. They walked around the stage with long sticks imitating rifles and singing the following lines to the tune of Bizet's *L'Arlesienne*:

Raz, dwa, trzy,
Koniec naszej gry,
Czas pożegnać się już z wami,
"Do widzenia" za drutami.

Cztery, pięć, sześć,
Nosimy dobrę wieść,
Że wyrosną znowu kwiaty
Gdy uciekną stąd psubraty.

Eins, zwei, drei,
Morgen sind wir frei,
Gdy ten bajzel w gruzy runie,
Każdy z nas jak ptak wyfrunie.

One, two, three,
The play is finished,
It's time to say "good-bye,"
We'll meet on the other side.

Four, five, six,
We bring you good tidings,
Flowers will grow here again
When the sons of bitches run away.

One, two, three,
Tomorrow we are free,
Once the mess here falls apart,
Each of us will fly out like a bird.

My play was a success, and it was shown not only in the Polish but also in several non-Polish blocks. However, its performance was plagued by mishaps. The second time around, the actor playing the Russian boatman became sick, and I, with my hoarse throat, had to deliver "Volga, Volga" in a raspy and barely audible voice; I did not regain my voice for several months. For our third performance, we were about to start the show in a French block when the fellow playing Hamlet collapsed on the stage. People murmured that he fainted because he took his role too much to heart, whereas in fact he was a very sick man. He was taken to the hospital right after the play, and a few days later he was dead. *Our* Hamlet never returned to his homeland. His role was taken over by somebody who had to read the words from a written page.

We performed the musical for several weeks, and I had already started to make up a new play when events on the outside caught up with us. On the first of February, the Americans broke through the Siegfried line, and on the ninth, they bombed Weimar, destroying its Gustloff Werke and some major ammunition dumps. A number of Buchenwald inmates died in the raid, and the SS mobilized new columns of workers to replace the dead and to remove the rubble in the streets. Through the grapevine we learned about the bombing of Dresden. These events had both an uplifting and a depressing effect. Like animals aroused to an impending danger, we could sense the tension and nervousness of the SS, who, without changing their outward behavior, looked at us with increasing hatred and suspicion. To them we were as guilty for their new woes as the squadrons of planes that turned their cities into rubble. We had no illusions that those who had built the camp in order to destroy us were not going to go down without dragging us along into the grave. Nor were we reassured by the stories that were brought to us by the transports arriving from the camps in the east. A number of minor camps were completely destroyed. Some trainloads had gotten stuck in the snow, with their cargoes starving or freezing to death. Himmler had issued an order to the *Lagerführer* that no inmate must fall alive into the hands of the Allied troops.

It was at the beginning of March that things got really bad. A spirit of foreboding hovered over the camp like the heavy mist that hung immobile over the Appelplatz. The nervousness and fear of the unpredictable took hold even of the patients in my block. The seriously ill closed their eyes and died, while the less sick wanted to leave their beds to return to their blocks to be, as they said, with their own. Most puzzling was the breakdown of the solidarity that had formed over the years among members of the various national groups. It was as if people suddenly realized that they could trust only their own kind, and that anyone speaking a foreign language would let them down. Men of the same block or nationality began to huddle together, forming little groups and whispering secrets to each other that no outsider was permitted to know.

Since everyone was convinced that we would not get out of the camp alive, people were dreaming up schemes of how they should fight or try to save themselves before the moment of reckoning arrived. Some plotted quietly, like men in a shipwreck ready to fight to the death for the last lifeboat, while others spent evenings planning the strategy of an armed defense. Both sides were, of course, utterly naïve: Buchenwald offered no feasible routes of escape, and the inmates had no arms that could stand up to the machine guns, watchtowers, and tanks of the SS. There was, of course, a third group, the group comprising the majority of the inmates, who were ready to wait passively until the very end. This was the group that hoped that the miracle of liberation would appear in the form of American tanks.

The first two groups were in the meantime busy indeed.

A mysterious activity seemed to go on in my own block. Around the middle of March I became aware that the two Czech medics who used to entertain themselves in the evening by playing chess or receiving their Czech friends suddenly disappeared, though I had not seen them leave the block. (The door to the block was near my *Schreibstube.*) What was even more peculiar was that their visitors had disappeared with them. After an hour or two they reappeared with blackened hands and dark smudges on their faces. It was clear that they were building some underground tunnel or bunker. When I asked them to show me the place, they said that they would do so in due time. In the meantime, they said, the place must remain a secret, and, anyway, it was too small to admit more than two or three of their Czech friends. When I told them that they were wasting their own and their friends' time, they called me a fool and said, "We shall see who was right."

More serious was the activity of the militant group, the one that was planning to fight. Most of its activity unfolded in Pathologie, and I learned from my friend about the kinds of weapons that were being prepared. Most of them were knives of various sizes and hatchets that inmates had managed to fashion in their workshops and smuggle into the camp. Mysteriously, they also acquired a number of pistols and several rifles, which they buried in various places in the camp. Right after the liberation I saw several German and Russian inmates with red armbands parade with these weapons, as if they were toys, although a day or two later they were confiscated by the American MPs. The acquisition of these toys must have cost Pathologie a substantial amount of booze and God knows how many cakes of exquisite soap. The only truly valuable possession of that group was its shortwave radio, which enabled its members to obtain the latest news from the front and, more important, to transmit messages to the approaching Allied troops. This radio must have saved thousands of lives. The same cannot be said about the arms, although several years after our liberation a number of Soviet and East European publications and memoirs about the camp began to disseminate the canard that Buchenwald was liberated by the inmates before the arrival of the Americans. The story of that heroism, spread for political ends, was pure fantasy.

The Liberation

At the end of March, Patton's Third Army crossed the Weser and Werre Rivers, took the city of Eisenach (about sixty miles from Weimar), and was pressing its way toward the east. We knew that our time had come, though we couldn't know what it was still going to cost us in lives.

The drama of our liberation lasted exactly eleven days, from Sunday, April 1st, until Wednesday, April 11th. On April 12th we observed on the old Appelplatz, behind lines of American soldiers, Roosevelt's memorial service.

On April 1st the roll call was, for the first time in the history of the camp, shifted from six to eight in the morning. Since it was a Sunday, only a few outfits left the camp for work in the SS kitchens and barracks. The tension increased on Monday when the roll call began again at eight, rather than at six, and when the columns were ordered to return to the blocks. The SS was apparently getting ready for some action. On the same day *Lagerführer* Pister summoned the *kapos* of the German blocks to warn them that the foreigners were going to attack the German inmates. He claimed to have intercepted a secret message in which Czech and French inmates had asked the approaching Americans to drop them arms with which to attack the Germans. He offered to get all the German inmates out of the camp, but none of them believed him, and none of them budged. On April 3rd there was no roll call, and no food was delivered to the camp; it was only the next day that some provisions were brought in.

On April 5th the evacuation of the camp began. The first to be evacuated were the Jews. The SS rounded up the Little Camp and block 22 and marched them out under heavy escort in three groups. Many of the guards wore the black uniforms of the Ukrainian and Vlasovite troops. On this day the camp again became *judenrein*, having lost more than eight thousand Jews. Those of us in the hospital followed the evacuation with bated breath, though by the evening we were the first to learn what had happened to many of the men on their march: they were brought back to the little plaza outside block 61 with bullet holes in their necks, fore-heads, and chests. When the number of corpses began to pile up in the little square and the boys of the *Totenkommando* failed to show up, we de-cided to take matters in our own hands by finding a wagon and trans-porting the corpses to a place near the crematorium. Needless to say, the crematorium too had ceased to work.

On April 6th the intercom ordered the inmates to step out on the Appelplatz for the roll call. Despite the assurance that nothing was going to happen, no one dared to step out. An hour or two later the in-tercom read out a list of forty-six inmates who were to present them-selves at the Kommendantur. This was a list of German and Austrian prisoners (several of them *kapos*) who had spent many of their best years in the camps. Among them was also the name of my friend and savior, August Kohn. But again, none of them stepped forth.

The next morning the SS invaded a number of blocks, chasing out their inhabitants with whips, machine guns, and barking dogs. In this way they gathered around ten thousand men and sent them on their march. Rumor had it that they were to march toward Dachau. To avoid a similar unpleasant encounter with the nervous and half-drunk SS, some blocks decided to organize themselves and to leave voluntarily at the next call. On the morning of April 8th, however, an American recon-naissance plane appeared over the camp, and the SS sounded the air raid alarm. By noon they were ready to go into action and again called on the blocks to step out on the Appelplatz. Still everybody stuck to the safety of his block. To avoid a massacre, the *kapos* reported to the Kommendan-tur that the inmates were afraid of an American air raid. In the meantime the people in the Pathologie transmitted a telegram to Patton's Third Army: "K. Z. Buchenwald SOS. Send help. They want to evacuate us and liquidate us." The army's headquarters sent an immediate answer: "Hold out. We are rushing to help you."

On April 10th, the SS, armed as before with whips and machine guns, surrounded the Czech, Polish, and French blocks. To their surprise, the entire blocks stepped out on the Appelplatz, forming columns of about twenty thousand men. Under heavy escort they too marched out from the camp. By that time the camp had lost about forty thousand men. Before nightfall a number of them were returned: dirty, covered with mud, in clothes torn by dogs, and mostly with bullets in their heads. And as before, the boys in my block jumped into action, removing the corpses. Only our two Czech medics refused to give us a hand. Nor did they repair to the bunker they had been building for several weeks. "It is all useless," they said. "There is no way out. Don't you see that they do not touch the hospitals, because they cannot force dying and sick people to set out on a march. But it is all useless because they will certainly dynamite the hospitals to prevent them from falling into the Allied hands. Yes, we'll have to die heroically, together with our sick."

On the night of the 10th we did not sleep well, and our nervousness was transmitted to the patients, who groaned and begged for help more than on any other night. On Wednesday morning I stepped out from the block and could hardly believe my eyes: some watchtowers stood empty, and I saw a guard in a black uniform (without a gun) slinking away from a tower. At seven in the morning the intercom broadcast the command: "Alle SS Truppen sofort aus dem Lager" (All SS troops abandon the camp right away).

At that point I knew that we were free.

With dozens of other inmates I stood close by the barbed wires that encircled the camp, looking out to the highway that led to Erfurt and was but a kilometer or so away from the camp. Then suddenly, on the horizon and growing with each minute, appeared tank after tank, tank after tank, moving like an unstoppable caterpillar—the most memorable sight of my life. Somebody shouted that the barbed wires were no longer electrified, and like a swarm of locusts we tore through the wires, running toward the road. We ran through a huge field toward the moving tanks, shouting all the way "Hurrah, hurrah!" and "America, America!" and the soldiers from their turrets threw us chocolate bars and biscuits.

In the afternoon of the same day, American officers in jeeps arrived in the camp. They came to my block to look at the sick, and I led them to the pile of corpses we had deposited over the last few days near the crematorium. Then they cordoned off the area, waiting for higher brass to take in the sight. The following day they brought a number of humble German citizens to visit the place. They came from Erfurt and Weimar and from the surrounding villages, and they claimed that they never knew what was going on high up on that mountain. They held handkerchiefs to their mouths, covered their faces with their hands, and now and then shed a few tears. They assured the American officers and soldiers that they didn't know, they just didn't know . . . What else could one expect them to say? They were all middle-aged folk, solid German burgers, and they themselves were certainly not responsible for the rotting piles of the dead.

Also on the 12th of April we attended the funeral service commemorating Roosevelt. There were speeches I could not quite hear or understand, the raising and lowering of the American flag, and some bugle blowing. The ceremony was impressive for its dignity and brevity. But I was most impressed by the American soldier. He was a military specimen I had never encountered before. The Polish, German, or Russian soldiers I had come across in my life had all moved with those angular movements that one associates with the wind-up wooden soldiers sold on street corners and that are developed through years of obedience and blind subordination. The American soldier stood on our Appelplatz relaxed, with a rifle at his side and an air of confidence that comes from a battle won and the righteousness of his cause. This, I thought, was an army for which I would like to work.

An Epilogue of Sorts

Three days after the liberation I left the camp with a document retrieved from the SS archives stating my identity, the place of my arrest, and the time I had spent in the camp. I left with my Polish friend Stefan, who, like me, had worked in one of the camp's *Reviers.* We hitched a ride on an American jeep and went down to the city of Erfurt, a charming medieval town with a number of old churches and a splendid cathedral. Our goal was to find the military outfit number 58, which was charged by the American authorities with organizing the Displaced Persons (DP) camps. These camps were formed to gather in all the slave laborers who had been brought to Germany to till the fields and produce the supplies for the German military machine. At the head of the outfit was a certain Major Collins, a professional soldier with a Texas accent. We offered ourselves as interpreters without pay and were hired on the spot because the outfit was going to deal with people from all parts of Europe. I became the major's personal interpreter, while Stefan, who had a better knowledge of French than of English, was assigned to the outfit's captain.

My major was probably a better soldier than organizer. Strictly speaking, he did not know a thing about refugees or camps, and it is lucky that he had a few smart soldiers under his command. They handled all the technical matters, beginning with the building of the camp, the housing of the people, and the ordering of provisions. A favorite occupation of the major was visiting the neighboring villages and towns to negotiate with local mayors for the delivery of certain goods to the camps. I must say that in these negotiations I played an important role, not only as an interpreter but also as a moderator. Major Collins had the strange habit of approaching each encounter with a gun in his hand, causing his interlocutors to stutter and tremble until the end of the meeting. It was obvious that Major Collins did not much care for the local mayors. Nor was he particularly fond of American blacks. At one time we visited a camp occupied by a black garrison. Before entering the camp he warned me that I should brace myself for the pungent smell of the black soldier. And he talked to them the way one talks to children. However, to Stefan and me he took a genuine liking. He set us up in an apartment in town, invited us to eat in the officers' mess, and treated us like members of his own outfit.

It was with regret that Stefan and I left outfit number 58 and the city of Erfurt. This came about near the end of June, when control of the town was turned over to the Russian army. My major asked me to take part in the solemn meeting accomplishing this transfer. The American representative was a skinny but elegant colonel, while the Russians were represented by a broad-shouldered and pudgy general, whose medals, like so many glittering stars, covered his chest all the way to his belly button. I don't recall what the discussion was all about (nor did it much matter, since the division of Germany had long before been settled at Yalta), but I remember that the Russian general insisted that I tell the American for which battles and river crossings he had won all these medals.

From Erfurt we moved to Frankfurt and Mannheim. Our services as interpreters were not much needed, since the organization of the DP camps was taken over by the United Nations Relief and Rehabilitation Administration (UNRRA), with its professional personnel and teams of young German secretaries. For a short while we worked for an inane British officer who made it his business to keep up the morale of the refugees by talking to any person he met. Since he knew only English, he insisted on having me or Stefan, or the two of us, always at his side. He was a doddering old bore, whereas the people we talked to had come from all parts of Europe and had interesting stories to tell. Some of them, especially those from the Baltic countries, were terribly afraid of the Russians and wished that the war were still going on, this time against the Russians. The Czechs and the Poles dreamed of going to America, while the Frenchmen were all eager to return home. The Russians were the first to be shipped back home, though many of them hid or ran over to the British zone. It seemed that none of them wanted to return to Russia.

Since we were not paid for our work and had very little to do, we spent much time visiting the countryside, flirting with the German girls or hanging around with other DPs. In this way we spent about five or six boring and meaningless months. Then one day, at the end of the year, a convoy of Polish soldiers arrived with truckloads of oranges and assorted gifts for the Polish children in the camps. The gifts were from the Second Polish Corps of General Anders, which had suffered terrible losses in the battle for Monte Cassino. It so happened that one of the officers of the convoy was Stefan's brother, who had fought with the Second Corps throughout the entire Italian campaign. After some deliberation it was decided that Stefan and I would join the convoy on its return to Italy. Thus I finally got a chance to visit one of the countries of my youthful dreams, not knowing that I would spend almost four years there.

The Polish outfit was stationed in a hilly little town overlooking the Adriatic, with real palm trees undulating in the Mediterranean breeze. However, I was more impressed by the poverty of its people than by the charm of the town. At noon when we sat down to eat, there was always a group of young boys who came by to look at us and to pick up the crumbs and handouts. Some of them were pimping for their not-much-older sisters, who could be had for a loaf of bread or a bar of soap. I noticed the same poverty after Stefan and I moved to the city of Trani in the south. For the Italians, 1946 was still a hard year. Stefan and I were much better off as guests of the Polish outfit; it had plenty of food and hard liquor and the two of us made several trips to the neighboring towns. On one such outing I saw Arezzo for the first time and the paintings of Piero della Francesca. However, every good story comes to an end. Toward the end of March we were informed by the commander of the post that the Second Corps could not go on forever feeding two able-bodied civilians. But at the same time he told us of a Polish *gymnasium* in Trani sponsored by General Anders that might be willing to take us on. In this way we could get our upkeep together with our education. I realized, not for the first time, that in order to eat I must go to school.

The school accepted us without any ado. On the basis of our age, experience, and sophistication (none of the students was expected to present a certificate of his or her previous education) we were admitted to the class that was scheduled to receive the *matura* at the end of the school year, in mid-June. This was clearly an accelerated course, but, after six years of war, Poland was badly in need of a new educated class.

The teachers, as well as the students, were a motley group that had

converged upon Trani through a variety of routes. Some had traveled
with the Second Corps all the way from Siberia, Persia, and the Near
East; some had come from Germany and France; and some were refugees
from the new People's Poland. The spirit of the school was ardently patriotic, strongly Catholic, and perversely anti-Semitic. This was true
more of the students than of the faculty, and I could not figure out where
such young people (especially the boys) had picked up the venomous
bug of anti-Semitism. The faculty was divided: the professor of history
and the school priest had taken a dislike to me from the first day they had
met me, a dislike I attributed to my suspiciously Jewish looks. But the director of the school, a certain Mr. Czernik, was a liberal and a poet; he
was quite fond of me, and I was sure that he saw to it that by the end of
the semester I won the school's first literary prize. Another friend of
mine—a true liberal known as "the Senator"—was our professor of Latin;
he was convinced that socialism might be beneficial for postwar Poland.
He probably never imagined what a calamity the Soviet-imposed socialism of the fifties would turn out to be for exhausted Poland. In my class,
and apparently in the whole school, there was only one Jew, a fellow
named Merfel, who told me about his Jewishness in deepest secrecy. He
was the first Jew I had met since the liberation of Buchenwald. He spoke
Polish with a Russian accent, for he and his parents had spent the war
somewhere in Siberia. Now they were settled in a Jewish DP camp in
Santa Cesarea (at the bottom of the Italian boot), waiting for a chance to
emigrate to America.

At the end of the school year the *gymnasium* closed, waiting with the
rest of the Second Corps to be evacuated to England. Some members of
the corps managed to settle permanently in England, but the majority
dispersed to all parts of the world (though mostly to North and South
America and to Australia). Very few chose to return to Poland.

Right after graduation we were visited by a young Polish priest, who
invited some of our boys to continue their higher education in Spain at
the expense of Franco's government. For some reason he never approached me with this proposal. By this time I had already decided to
follow Merfel to the Jewish camp, to return to my "tribe." After the last

three years I was tired of being a Catholic and a "pure" Pole. I parted
ways with my school colleagues without any qualms, though I found it
painful to say goodbye to Stefan and even more painful to separate from
Teresa, my girlfriend of the last three months and the muse who had inspired the theme of my poems and their heartfelt, brooding, and pulsat-
ing beat. But my muse felt she should return to her husband, who was a
flier in the Polish squadron in England, and from whom she had been
separated by the vicissitudes of war. For a whole year I couldn't get her
out of my mind. I would see her smile in some of the paintings by Botti-
celli, hear her whisper in the fountains of Rome, and smell her hair in the
oranges that I bought at the Campo dei Fiori.

With the Polish *maturas* in our pockets, Merfel and I took the train to
Santa Cesarea, where the remnants of Eastern European Jewry had set up
their temporary tents, waiting to be admitted to Palestine or to any other
non-Communist country that would take them. In reality the "tents"
were a large number of Quonset huts with tin roofs that sizzled in the
summer's southern sun, with primitive plumbing and a fair share of mos-
quitoes. On the other hand, there was a magnificent beach and kitchens
that provided ample and relatively decent food. More than a thousand
people milled around in the camp with nothing much to do except play
dominos and cards or lie on the beach. Happiest of all were the young
Jewish boys who would climb up the towering dark rocks at one end of
the beach and plunge recklessly into the dark blue sea. Another group
that kept itself busy were the radical Zionists (the supporters of Irgun),
who exercised each morning, sang nationalistic Hebrew songs, and
spoke of the promise of a great Jewish state. Their number gradually and
imperceptibly shrank, as some of them boarded ships to be smuggled il-
legally into the Holy Land.

The mood of the majority was hardly upbeat. Having lost their
physical and emotional bonds with the past and being faced with an unpredictable future, they were like people for whom the clocks had
stopped. In fact, they were living less with hope than with suppressed or
loudly expressed resentments against the villains of this world: against
the Russians for having put them to work like criminals in the camps,

against the Poles for staging pogroms against the returning Jews, against the Americans for refusing to open their gates, and against the British for denying them the homeland promised them by God. In this atmosphere of boredom, expectation, and frustration, I myself began to feel trapped, useless, and old (I was almost twenty-six). For where was I heading and what was I going to do with my life? In this mood I wrote what was to be one of my last Polish poems:

Ludziom, co spieszą wiecznie bezdomni,
do domów dzieciństwa, do cichych zaułków,
szarość sufitów i murów przypomni,
że nigdy nie znajdą dla serca przytułku.

Ludziom, co gonią trwożnie przez miasto,
by oprzeć wzrok na ojców wlasności,
uderzy w twarz framug i mebli kanciastość
i zgrzyt zegarów się na nich rozzłości.

Ludziom, co w ciszy własnego ogniska
szukają schronienia od życia zawiei,
gładkość biurek, wężowa i śliska,
zatruje ostatnie źródla nadziei.

Ludziom, którzy sie cieszą, jak dzieci,
ze uszli cało po wielkiej klęsce,
krzywizna luster twarze zeszpeci,
i w próżni bezwladnie opadną ręce.

People who forever homeless
hurry through quiet lanes to the homes of their childhood,
will be reminded by the grayness of the ceilings and walls,
that their hearts will never find a place of rest.

People who timidly move through the city
to rest their sight on the property of their fathers,

will be hit in the face by the edginess of the window sills and furniture
and the clocks will angrily grind their teeth at them.

People who in the quiet of their hearth
seek refuge from the turmoil of life,
will have their last sources of hope poisoned
by the slippery, serpentine smoothness of their desks.

People who are cheerful, like children,
that they got out with their lives from the great disaster,
will find their faces distorted in crooked mirrors,
and their hands will fall down helpless in a void.

But in this world of accidents, a lucky break came once more. I learned
through the grapevine that the Joint Distribution Committee was about
to offer fellowships to any Jewish student studying at an Italian university. At the end of August I took a train to Rome, passed the qualifying
Italian exams in one of the local high schools, and entered the university.
And thus I returned again to the portals of learning for the sake of secur-
ing a meal. The fellowship was about ten thousand lire a month, suffi-
cient for four or five dinners. But in time, I got myself some part-time
jobs (including the teaching of Latin in a Joint-sponsored Jewish high
school), and I somehow survived, learned, and grew. At the end of 1949
I immigrated to the United States.

GLOSSARY OF MENTIONED
WRITERS AND SCHOLARS

Boy Żeleński, Tadeusz (1874–1941): Poet, theatrical critic, and outstanding translator of French literature. His poetry was much admired for its wit and verbal virtuosity.

Czernik, Stanisław (1899–1969): Author of poems and stories written about, and in the style of Polish "peasant" literature; all published in postwar Poland.

Fefer, Itsik (1900–1952): Promoter of the Communist Party line in life and in most of his otherwise skillful and rhythmically lulling lyrical verse. Shot with other Soviet Yiddish writers in August 1952.

Hofshteyn, Dovid (1889–1952): The most gifted of the Soviet Yiddish poets. Spent some time in Palestine where he wrote in Hebrew and Yiddish. His poems are captivating for their lyricism and metrical inventiveness. Executed with other Soviet Yiddish writers in August 1952.

Imber, Samuel (1889–1943?): Author of lyrical poetry in Hebrew, Yiddish, and Polish and an acerbic political polemicist (in Polish). Died with his pianist wife in one of the German raids in a small Eastern Galician town.

Jan Zygmunt (1909–1979): His actual surname was Jakubowski. After the war he returned to Poland, where he wrote and edited books on nineteenth- and twentieth-century Polish literature. For a while, he was dean at Warsaw University.

Kuncewiczowa, Maria (1859–1975?): Author of several novels marked by refined lyricism. In the 60s, she taught Polish literature at the University of Chicago.

Kvitko, Leyb (1890–1952): Poet and editor of Yiddish literary journals. Best known for his children's poems and stories that were translated into many languages of the Soviet Union. Executed with other Soviet Yiddish writers in August 1952.

Manger, Itsik (1901–1969): For the lyrical, playful, and folklorist quality of his verse, Manger became known as the troubadour of modern Yiddish poetry. In his witty biblical cycles, he infuses new life into the Old Testament themes and patriarchal figures. After the war, he settled in Israel.

Markish, Peretz (1895–1952): An immensely talented lyrical poet, novelist, and playwright. After spending some time in France and Palestine, he returned to Russia in 1926 and became a dedicated supporter of the Soviet state, a move that did not save him from the firing squad in August 1952.

Norwid, Cyprian (1821–1883): Painter, playwright, and poet, he expanded the verbal and metrical possibilities of Polish verse. Neglected in his lifetime, he was rediscovered at the beginning of the twentieth century. He rates now as one of the giants of Polish literature.

Polak, Edmund (1914–1978?): Author and translator of several hundred poems, plays, and songs written in Auschwitz and Buchenwald, most of them preserved in a Warsaw national museum. In 1968, he published *Morituri*, a memoir of his experiences in the camps.

Putrament, Jerzy (1910–1986): Poet, novelist, and early supporter of Communist causes and of the Soviet Union. Opposed the trend toward liberalization and a freer Polish press. Served as Polish ambassador in Switzerland and in France.

Rawicz, Piotr (1919–1982): After a period of wanderings on the Aryan side, he was caught by the SS and sent to Auschwitz, which he survived as a Ukrainian national. In 1947 he settled in Paris, where he continued his studies of Sanskrit for a while. He gained critical acclaim through two semiautobiographical novels written in French:

Le Sang du Ciel and *Le compagnon d'un Singe*. He committed suicide in 1982.

Schutz, Bruno (1892–1942): Painter and writer of surrealist Polish prose. Was shot by a German officer during a raid in his hometown, Drohobycz, in 1942. His reputation as a master of the modernist short story was established after the fall of the Polish communist regime.

Shimmel, Moyshe (1903–1942): Like some other Galician Jews, began writing in Polish to switch later to Yiddish. His poetry is marked by a fluid lyricism and a musical tilt.

Shudrikh, Jakov (1906–1943): Published several slim volumes of verse that gained him the reputation of a proletarian poet. In reality, his poetry was marked by a feeling of unredeemed pessimism. He died in 1943 in his hometown of Lwów in a firefight with the SS.

Słonimski, Antoni (1895–1976): Poet, comedy writer, and publicist. Cofounder (with Tuwim) of the leading interwar literary circle Skamander. Spent the war years in the West to return to Poland in 1951. His *Oda do Młodych* (Ode to the Young) was a harbinger of the so-called Polish thaw.

Stiffel, Frank (1917–): Studied medicine in Belgium and French philology in Lwów, where he helped form a group of young Polish writers. Escaped to the Aryan side in 1942 and was betrayed and sent to Auschwitz. His book about the Holocaust, *The Tale of the Ring: A Kaddish*, was highly praised.

Tuwim, Julian (1894–1953): The leading poet in interwar Poland, he was also a great satirist and translator (mostly from Russian). Cofounded (with Słonimski) the literary group Skamander. During the war years abroad (including New York), he wrote the epic-lyrical poem *Kwiaty Polskie* (Polish Flowers), a masterpiece of modern Polish literature.

Unbegaun, Boris (1878–1973): A Slavist of Baltic German origin, he wrote on Russian and the South Slavic languages and literatures. He taught at Strassbourg, Oxford, and in the United States.

Vasmer, Max (1886–1962): Noted German Slavist, professor at Berlin University. He was the author of works on Slavic ethnogenesis and onomastics and of a monumental Russian etymological dictionary.

Vogel, Deborah (1902–1942): Daughter of a distinguished assimilated Jewish family in Lwów, she had but a rudimentary knowledge of spoken Yiddish, yet produced several slim volumes of Yiddish avant-garde poetry.

Waslilewska, Wanda (1903–1964): Daughter of a distinguished member of the Polish Socialist Party (PPS), she started out as a socialist, but in time became a communist firebrand and strong supporter of the Soviet Union. Her novels are largely a reflection of her political views. In 1945, she married the Ukranian writer Kornijchuk and settled in Kiev.

Wyspiański, Stanisław (1869–1907): Poet, playwright, and painter. He is best known for his social and patriotic plays, and especially for his play *Wesele* (The Wedding) set in the social and artistic ambience of his native Cracow.

Zieliński, Tadeusz (1859–1944): Outstanding classical philologist. Taught at the Universities of St. Petersburg and Warsaw and wrote about Greek and Roman Literatures, languages, cultures, and religions.